The Taurus Book
Everything You Should Know About Tauruses

CRAFTED BY SKRIUWER

Copyright © 2025 by Skriuwer.

All rights reserved. No part of this book may be used or reproduced in any form whatsoever without written permission except in the case of brief quotations in critical articles or reviews.

At **Skriuwer**, we're more than just a team—we're a global community of people who love books. In Frisian, "Skriuwer" means "writer," and that's at the heart of what we do: creating and sharing books with readers worldwide. Wherever you are in the world, **Skriuwer** is here to inspire learning.

Frisian is one of the oldest languages in Europe, closely related to English and Dutch, and is spoken by about **500,000 people** in the province of **Friesland** (Fryslân), located in the northern Netherlands. It's the second official language of the Netherlands, but like many minority languages, Frisian faces the challenge of survival in a modern, globalized world.

We're using the money we earn to promote the Frisian language.

For more information, contact : **kontakt@skriuwer.com** (www.skriuwer.com)

TABLE OF CONTENTS

CHAPTER 1: UNDERSTANDING TAURUS

- Basic nature and traits of Taurus
- Role of astrology in defining Taurus
- Common misconceptions and initial insights

CHAPTER 2: TAURUS SYMBOL AND TRAITS

- Bull as the main symbol of Taurus
- Steadiness, reliability, and calm approach
- How the symbol shapes Taurus's overall reputation

CHAPTER 3: TAURUS IN ASTROLOGY BASICS

- How Taurus fits into the zodiac wheel
- Significance of birth charts and planetary aspects
- Fixed sign qualities and earth element influence

CHAPTER 4: TAURUS ELEMENT AND PLANET

- Earth element's grounding effects
- Venus as the ruling planet and its impact
- Blending comfort, beauty, and practicality

CHAPTER 5: STRENGTHS OF TAURUS

- Dependability and loyalty
- Patience, persistence, and consistent effort
- Appreciation for sensory pleasures and tangible results

CHAPTER 6: WEAKNESSES OF TAURUS

- Stubborn tendencies and resistance to change
- Overattachment to comfort or routine
- Balancing practicality with flexibility

CHAPTER 7: TAURUS IN FRIENDSHIPS

- Approach to forming and keeping friends
- Loyalty and calm presence in social circles
- Navigating conflicts and building long-term bonds

CHAPTER 8: TAURUS IN FAMILY LIFE

- Roles as children, siblings, parents, or partners
- Desire for stability and harmony at home
- Conflict resolution and creating a supportive environment

CHAPTER 9: TAURUS IN WORK LIFE

- Preferred job settings and steady work habits
- Taurus as an employee, teammate, or leader
- Handling deadlines, stress, and workplace changes

CHAPTER 10: TAURUS AND MONEY

- Financial security and budgeting styles
- Attitude toward saving, spending, and comfort
- Balancing material needs with deeper fulfillment

CHAPTER 11: TAURUS AND OTHER SIGNS

- Interactions with fire, air, water, and other earth signs
- Potential harmony and challenges in partnerships
- Finding common ground in different zodiac relationships

CHAPTER 12: CARING FOR YOURSELF AS A TAURUS

- Physical and emotional self-care habits
- Healthy boundaries and personal routines
- Embracing comfort while avoiding unhealthy extremes

CHAPTER 13: TAURUS AND DAILY HABITS

- Morning and evening routines for calm
- Effective ways to maintain structure without boredom
- Balancing steady habits with small changes

CHAPTER 14: MYTHS ABOUT TAURUS

- Common stereotypes and their origins
- Nuanced realities behind oversimplifications
- Taurus beyond the usual labels

CHAPTER 15: TAURUS AND PASTIMES

- Preferred hobbies and interests
- Love for creative, sensory, or nature-based activities
- Finding joy and relaxation in everyday pleasures

CHAPTER 16: TAURUS IN DIFFERENT CULTURES

- Global perspectives on bull symbolism
- Parallels between Taurus and various cultural myths
- Shared themes of strength and stability worldwide

CHAPTER 17: TAURUS IN ART AND STORIES

- Historical depictions of the bull in art and literature
- Modern portrayals emphasizing Taurus qualities
- Symbolic lessons drawn from bull imagery

CHAPTER 18: TAURUS OVER TIME

- Evolution of Taurus from ancient to modern eras
- Influence of scientific shifts and cultural changes
- Why Taurus remains relevant across centuries

CHAPTER 19: TAURUS AND SUITABLE PLACES

- Ideal home environments and travel spots
- Balancing urban life with a need for calm
- Cultivating cozy, grounded settings for well-being

CHAPTER 20: COMMON QUESTIONS ABOUT TAURUS

- Addressing frequent queries about personality and habits
- Practical tips for living or working with Taurus
- Reinforcing Taurus's core themes of calm, comfort, and stability

CHAPTER 1: UNDERSTANDING TAURUS

Taurus is one of the zodiac signs found in astrology. Astrology is a way people look at the stars and planets to find patterns that some believe can say something about people's personalities and behaviors. The zodiac is made up of twelve different signs, and each sign covers a period of time in the year. Taurus takes place each year from about April 20 to May 20. If a person is born during these dates, they are often seen as a Taurus. Some people feel that being a Taurus can show them a few things about themselves, such as how they see the world, how they might act, and how they feel most comfortable in life.

But what does it really mean to be a Taurus? Many people say that Taurus is a sign linked with steadiness and practicality. A Taurus might like to have security and feel safe in many parts of life, such as family, money, and day-to-day routines. Some people also say that Taurus can be quite calm and consistent, and they do not like to change their ways too quickly. This is because Taurus is often described as reliable. Yet, there is more to it than that. A person who is a Taurus might also like comfort and nice things, whether that is good food, a cozy blanket, or a pretty piece of art. These small pleasures can be very important to someone who is a Taurus.

Since many people are curious about what makes Taurus special, this book is focused on the different parts of Taurus, such as where it comes from, how people describe it, how it might show up in everyday life, and how it might link with other signs. These are only ideas and are not rules set in stone. Everyone is still their own person, with many different traits and choices that make them unique. Yet, some people feel that learning about Taurus can help them understand things about themselves or people they know who might be Taurus.

Introduction to the Zodiac and Taurus

To start understanding Taurus, it might be helpful to know a little about astrology and the zodiac. Astrology began a very long time ago, in ancient civilizations that used the movement of planets and stars as a way to track time and important events. Over time, people made a system of zodiac signs. Each sign is like a part of the sky, and the sun appears to pass through these parts during certain dates of the year.

If you see pictures of the zodiac, you will sometimes see that each sign has its own symbol, such as a lion for Leo or a crab for Cancer. Taurus is often shown as a bull. The bull is strong and persistent. Many people link the bull with the idea of standing firm, being steady, and having a strong will. These are traits that people often say belong to Taurus.

Each sign also has an element, such as fire, earth, air, or water. Taurus is an earth sign. The word "earth" here reminds us of the ground we stand on and the plants that grow in the soil. Because of this, Taurus is sometimes said to be closely connected to things like stability, patience, and practicality. This is because earth signs are often described as steady, like the ground beneath our feet. People who are Taurus might feel more comfortable in routines and in taking things step by step.

Why People Study Taurus

Some might ask: why do people even look at zodiac signs? For some, astrology is an interesting hobby. For others, it might be a more serious belief system or a way to think about life. There are also people who might look at their zodiac sign for fun, like checking horoscopes in a newspaper or online, just to see if they fit. But many find a sense of comfort or enjoyment in the idea that the stars and planets can have a little bit of meaning in their own life.

Taurus is a sign known for being steady and dependable. Many want to learn about this sign because they know a Taurus or they are a Taurus themselves. People might want to see if the traits they read about match what they see in real life. Does a Taurus friend really like calm settings and dislike sudden changes? Does a Taurus family member really enjoy cooking and having nice food around? These are the types of fun questions people ask when they read about Taurus.

Of course, not all individuals who are Taurus will be the same. Some will have other parts of their birth chart that lead them to act in ways that seem different from the usual ideas about Taurus. But many feel that looking at the main sign is a good place to start learning a little more about astrology.

Taurus in Daily Life

When people think about Taurus, one of the first words that might come to mind is "stability." This might mean that someone who is a Taurus likes to have a predictable schedule. They may enjoy waking up at the same time each morning, eating a favorite breakfast, and following a daily routine that does not change much. A Taurus might like to plan ahead and know what will happen next. When things in life become too chaotic, a Taurus can become stressed.

Taurus people might enjoy quiet moments at home where they can relax and feel at peace. They might like simpler things, like reading a favorite story or relaxing in a warm place. They often want to feel that everything around them is calm and steady. Sometimes, people say that Taurus might be resistant to change. This is not always a bad thing, as it might mean that a Taurus can keep going when things get tough. But it can also mean that if a big change happens, it might take a Taurus some time to adjust. They might not be the type who gets excited about changing their routine.

Many Taurus individuals are described as patient. If something is difficult, they might keep at it until they are done. They often do not want to rush tasks and would rather take their time. This can lead them to produce good work, whether it is a creative project or a job that must be done carefully. Sometimes, people describe Taurus as a sign that has a slow and steady pace. They prefer to take small steps, but each step is careful and thoughtful.

The Basic Personality of Taurus

When talking about any zodiac sign, people like to list a few traits or adjectives that are commonly said to fit that sign. For Taurus, some key words often used are:

1. **Steady** – A Taurus might not be quick to act or change, but once they begin, they keep going.

2. **Reliable** – Many believe that a Taurus is trustworthy and can be counted on to do what they say.

3. **Practical** – Taurus might choose the simplest or most realistic option, not wanting to waste resources.

4. **Comfort-Loving** – Taurus might prefer environments that make them feel warm, safe, or happy.

5. **Slow to Change** – Taurus might resist big changes or new ideas unless they can be sure they will benefit.

These traits are not meant to be strict rules. Instead, they are more like patterns that many people who are Taurus say fit them. If someone does not feel these traits match them, that is fine. Everyone is different, and astrology is just one way people like to look at personality traits.

Misunderstandings About Taurus

Sometimes people can hold certain ideas about Taurus that might not be completely correct or might be too general. For instance, a common misunderstanding is that Taurus is always lazy or does not want to do anything. This is not always true. While Taurus might enjoy relaxation, they can also be very hardworking. They just like to work at a pace that allows them to feel comfortable and sure about what they are doing. Once they commit to a project, they will try their hardest to see it through.

Another misunderstanding might be that a Taurus only cares about money or material things. While many Taurus individuals do appreciate security, which can include money, it is not the only thing that matters to them. They often enjoy good food, a comfortable home, or beautiful objects, but they might also care a lot about sharing with loved ones. The desire for comfort can be more about feeling safe and happy in a stable space than just having fancy things.

Taurus in Different Places and Times

People have looked at Taurus in many parts of the world. The sign has a long history in astrology and has roots in ancient civilizations. The bull symbol often appears in old stories, pictures, and myths that have existed in different cultures. The idea of the bull shows strength, determination, and stability. This is part of why Taurus is linked with these traits.

Around the world, you might find that people describe Taurus in ways that have much in common. Still, the words or pictures they use to describe it can differ based on culture. Sometimes, it is fun to see how groups of people in different countries have used the symbol of the bull to represent traits like strength and steadiness.

Why Taurus Matters to Some People

A person might find Taurus interesting because they see parts of themselves in the sign, or they might want to understand a friend or family member who is Taurus. Some people also think that looking at the traits of Taurus can help them handle problems in a calm, steady way. For example, if a person has a hard time finishing tasks, they might look at Taurus traits for advice on how to be consistent. If a person feels restless, they might like to adopt some of Taurus's calm and steady ways to help them feel more centered.

For many, the sign of Taurus is a reminder that things can take time and that steady effort can be very helpful. Rather than rushing, a Taurus approach might be to slow down, remain patient, and focus on one step at a time. This can be a useful reminder in a world that often feels very fast. While not everyone is a Taurus, the sign's emphasis on calmness can be used by anyone who wants to live life at a more measured pace.

Taurus and How It Fits into the Bigger Picture

Taurus is the second sign in the zodiac, coming right after Aries. Each sign in astrology is said to build on the lessons of the one before it. Aries is often seen as a spark of new beginnings, with lots of enthusiasm. Then Taurus comes along and says, "Now we must be practical. We must build something solid." This is how many people think of Taurus as the anchor that keeps things from floating away. Without Taurus, we might have lots of ideas but no way to make them happen. Taurus encourages slow and consistent work that leads to real results.

Following Taurus in the zodiac is Gemini, which adds an element of curiosity. So, Taurus stands as a moment of calm between the rush of Aries and the quick thinking of Gemini. This helps keep everything balanced. In astrology, every sign has its place, and Taurus's place is linked with steady development, safety, and support.

The Purpose of This Book

This book is made to explore all the different aspects of Taurus that people often find interesting. There will be discussions about the symbol of Taurus, the traits many people link to Taurus, how Taurus acts in friendships and family settings, and even how Taurus handles money. Each chapter will look at a specific part of Taurus. This can be helpful for people who want a deeper look into what it means to be a Taurus.

But it is good to remember that this is just a guide. It is not a set of strict rules for how to act or who to be. A person can be a Taurus and still do things or feel things that are not always linked with Taurus traits. We should always keep in mind that astrology is a way to look at ourselves, but it does not define us fully.

For now, know that Taurus is often linked with steady effort, a calm approach, and an appreciation for comfort. These ideas might help you if you are a Taurus or if you know someone who is a Taurus. When you understand these traits, you might see ways to interact better with yourself and others.

Helpful Tips for Reading About Taurus

Stay Open-Minded
 As you read, remember that people are unique. Not everyone with

the same zodiac sign will have the same behavior. Use these ideas as a broad picture, not a firm rule.

Look at the Positive and Negative
Taurus, like every zodiac sign, has qualities that can be seen as positive or negative depending on how you look at them. For example, being slow to act could be called patient or stubborn, depending on the situation. It is good to see both sides.

Use What Helps You
If you find helpful tips about staying patient or being consistent, feel free to use them. If something does not apply to you, you can let it go.

Remember Context
Not all signs express themselves in the same way. A Taurus who has grown up in a busy city might show the traits differently from a Taurus who grew up on a farm. Environment can matter a lot.

By keeping these thoughts in mind, you can get the most out of this book and learn more about Taurus in a way that feels practical.

CHAPTER 2: TAURUS SYMBOL AND TRAITS

The bull is the animal linked with Taurus. It is a powerful creature known for strength and patience. For many centuries, people have looked at bulls as symbols of toughness and the power to stand strong in one place. In the sky, the constellation of Taurus is supposed to look like the shape of a bull's head and horns. This image has stayed with us for a long time, and it helps us remember what many people feel is at the heart of Taurus: steady energy, stability, and a strong will.

But what else does this symbol mean, and how does it connect to the traits that people often talk about when they speak of Taurus? In this chapter, we will look at the bull symbol more closely, and we will also talk about the main traits that astrology experts often link with Taurus. We will see how these traits can appear in daily life.

The Bull as the Main Symbol

1. **Why a Bull?**
   The bull has long been seen as a strong and dependable animal in many parts of the world. Bulls are often associated with farming and working the land. This idea ties in well with Taurus as an earth sign. An earth sign is linked with themes of nature, solidity, and productivity. The bull is also known for a steady pace. It is not always fast, but it can keep going. This fits the idea of Taurus being patient and consistent.

2. **Constellation Story**
   If you look at the constellation of Taurus in the night sky, you

might spot a shape that resembles a bull's head with two horns sticking out. The ancient Greeks and other cultures had stories that linked this group of stars with a bull. While the exact myths can differ, the image of a strong bull in the sky has stayed with us. This gave rise to the zodiac sign we now call Taurus.

3. **Symbolic Qualities**

When people think of a bull, they often think of certain qualities. A bull can be stubborn when it wants to be, but it is also calm when left in peace. It can stand in a field, eating grass and not being bothered by much. But if something annoys the bull too much, it can charge forward with great force. This idea matches many people's descriptions of Taurus: calm most of the time, but ready to defend itself or its loved ones if pushed too far.

Key Traits Linked with Taurus

Stability and Persistence

Taurus is usually described as one of the most stable signs of the zodiac. When a Taurus person sets out to do something, they will keep going until it is finished. This persistence can be a strong point in many parts of life, from school to work to personal hobbies. It can help them achieve goals because they do not quit easily. They might take their time, but they often produce results.

Practical Outlook

Taurus tends to look at the real facts of a situation. Instead of dreaming about wild ideas, a Taurus will try to see what is actually possible. They often prefer choices that are sure and proven. This does not mean they cannot be creative. They can be, but they also want to see how that creativity can work in the real world. For example, if a Taurus loves painting, they might try to learn solid techniques and methods so they can produce art that matches what they imagine.

Value of Comfort

A common trait linked with Taurus is the love of comfort. This can mean enjoying good food, cozy clothes, or a nice place to rest. Taurus might also like items that feel smooth, smell good, or taste good. They might set up their home to be relaxing, with soft pillows or warm blankets. This love of comfort can also appear in how they handle relationships: they might prefer calm, peaceful interactions rather than stressful or unpredictable fights.

Reliability

Another notable Taurus trait is reliability. Many say that if a Taurus friend says they will help you, they will. If a Taurus worker promises to complete a project, they will do it. This sense of reliability can make Taurus people good friends, coworkers, or family members. They often want others to trust them, and they prefer to keep their word.

Strong-willed

Some might call Taurus stubborn, while others call them determined. This can be seen as a strength or a weakness, depending on the situation. If a Taurus believes in something, they will stand by it and push back against anyone who tries to sway them. This can be very helpful if they are fighting for a cause or working toward a goal. But it can also cause problems if they refuse to change their opinion even when faced with facts that say otherwise.

How These Traits Show Up Day to Day

Work Life

In a job, a Taurus might be the person you can rely on to show up on time and finish the tasks given to them. They might not be the loudest or the quickest worker, but they are steady. They often like jobs that have a clear structure and routine. This gives them a sense of security, which they find comforting. They might also like jobs where they can see real results, such as working with their hands or creating something tangible.

Home Life

At home, a Taurus might want peace and stability. They might like cooking meals that taste delicious and make the home smell nice. They might be the family member who keeps traditions like having the same favorite meal on a certain day, or watching a certain show every night. This consistency can help the entire household feel secure and at ease.

Personal Hobbies

Taurus might pick hobbies that allow them to enjoy their senses. For example, they may like gardening, painting, woodworking, or any hobby where they can feel and see what they have created. They also might enjoy quiet times at home with a good book or a comfortable seat. Again, it is about being consistent, calm, and connected to the real world.

Conflicts and Challenges

Even though Taurus has many strong points, it can also face certain problems because of its traits. One common issue is the stubborn streak. A Taurus might stick to a point of view long after everyone else has moved on. If they feel threatened or pressured, they might dig in and refuse to budge. This can cause arguments that last longer than needed.

Another challenge can be an unwillingness to accept new ideas or changes. If a Taurus is very set in their routine, they might find it hard to adapt to a sudden shift at work or in the family. They might feel stressed and could resist the change. Over time, learning to be more open can help them handle life's twists and turns more easily.

The Physical Symbol of Taurus

The zodiac symbol for Taurus is usually drawn as a circle with two horns on top. It looks like a small bull's head. This symbol appears in astrology charts and in horoscope sections. It is a simple way to show the idea of the bull. Some people wear this symbol on jewelry, clothing, or in art because they feel it reflects their Taurus identity.

The horns on the symbol stand for the bull's steady strength. This reminds people that Taurus is not easily moved. If you see the Taurus symbol next to someone's name, it means their sun sign is Taurus. In astrology, the sun sign is the main sign that many people know, but there are also moon signs and rising signs. For now, we are mostly focused on the sun sign, which is the usual way we talk about a person's zodiac identity.

Linking the Symbol to Everyday Behavior

The bull can be calm and peaceful, but if you make it angry, it can charge with power. The same goes for many Taurus individuals. They can be laid-back, but if they feel pushed, they might react strongly. This is sometimes called the "Taurus temper." Though they might not get angry quickly, once they do, it can be quite intense.

Taurus's connection to the earth can also appear in everyday life as a love for nature or the outdoors. Some Taurus people might enjoy taking care of plants, walking in forests, or spending time around mountains or bodies of water. This can help them feel grounded and at peace. Since the bull is also linked with farming and land, some Taurus individuals find real happiness in growing their own food or caring for animals.

How Taurus Traits Can Help Others

Taurus can be a source of comfort for friends or family members who are going through tough times. Their stable nature can help calm others. Because Taurus is reliable, they can be the person you call when you need someone to help you think in a practical way. They might say, "Let's look at the facts," or "Let's see what steps we can take." This calm, step-by-step approach can be soothing in times of trouble.

In group situations, the Taurus person might be the one who keeps everyone steady. If the group is struggling with stress, a Taurus might remind everyone to take it slow and be patient. They might also focus on making sure everyone is comfortable, such as picking a place to meet that feels welcoming.

Special Note on Taurus Sensitivity

Even though Taurus is often described as strong, that does not mean Taurus people do not have feelings. They can be quite sensitive inside, especially if someone they care about is hurting. Their love of comfort also means they can be gentle with others, wanting to give them a safe and cozy place to rest. This sensitivity can also appear in their relationships. They might not always say a lot of words about their feelings, but they show love through actions, like cooking meals, giving kind gifts, or offering a shoulder to lean on.

Balancing the Bull's Energy

If you are a Taurus or know someone who is, it can help to be aware of the balance between steadiness and stubbornness. Sometimes being steady is helpful, and sometimes it can hold you back if it stops you from accepting new things. A good practice for many Taurus individuals is to remember that change can be positive. It does not have to be scary. By reminding themselves of this, they can open the door to new experiences without losing their stable nature.

Another way to balance the bull's energy is to set small goals for trying new activities. Instead of a big shake-up in routine, a Taurus might feel more comfortable making a small change every once in a while. Over time, these small changes can add up and help the person grow without feeling too uneasy.

Exploring Taurus Traits in Depth

Strength
 A Taurus can be strong both physically (if they choose to work on it) and mentally (in terms of willpower). This strength is like the bull's power. It can be used to stand firm in difficult times.

Loyalty
 Taurus is often seen as very loyal. Once they care about someone, they will stand by them. This can make them good friends and partners. But if that trust is broken, a Taurus might hold a grudge for a long time.

Patience
 Being patient is a hallmark of Taurus. However, this does not mean they never get angry. It just means they have a high threshold before they explode. They might give many chances or wait a long time before showing frustration.

Resourcefulness
 Since Taurus is an earth sign, they often know how to use what is around them. They might prefer fixing an item rather than throwing it away and buying a new one. They like practical solutions that save time and resources.

Simplicity

Taurus might find joy in the little things. They could prefer a simple but tasty meal over a fancy dinner. They might like comfortable clothes instead of flashy outfits. This love of simplicity helps them remain calm.

Common Misunderstandings of the Bull Symbol

Always Angry

Some people might think the bull symbol means Taurus is angry or aggressive. This is not necessarily true. Taurus can be calm most of the time. Anger only shows up if they feel pushed too far.

Never Budges

Another misunderstanding is that Taurus can never change. While they may be slow to embrace big shifts, they can change if they see it as the best thing for them. The process might take longer, but it can happen.

All About Possessions

It is true that many Taurus individuals like nice things or a stable home. But they also have a caring side. They do not only care about objects; they care about people and experiences that help them feel safe and loved.

The Role of the Bull in Different Myths

Throughout history, the bull appears in many stories and myths worldwide. Although these myths can differ, many of them highlight the bull's strength and connection to nature. Some tales talk about bulls helping to grow crops or protect their land. Others show the bull as a fierce creature that must be respected. These stories feed into the ideas we have today about Taurus being a sign of stability, protection, and calm power.

Bringing It All Together

The symbol of the bull for Taurus is more than just an image. It is a way to understand the core nature that people often link with this sign. The bull reminds us of power that is steady rather than always quick. It can stand still for a long time, storing energy. This is how many Taurus individuals go through life, slowly building up their efforts until they are ready to act. Then, when they do act, they can move with a lot of energy and determination.

If you see someone with a small bull symbol on a necklace or in their home, it might mean they identify strongly with Taurus. Or it might just mean they like the image of the bull. But if they do identify with Taurus, it could be a sign they see themselves as steady, calm, and connected to the earth in some way.

Tips for Living with Taurus Traits

Embrace Your Steadiness
If you are a Taurus, remember that your slow and steady approach can help you do things well. Others might try to hurry you, but stay true to your careful pace.

Watch Out for Stubbornness
It is fine to stand firm in your beliefs, but try to stay open to the views of others. They might have good ideas that can help you.

Enjoy Comfort Wisely
Liking comfort is not a bad thing. But be careful not to get so used to comfort that you avoid growth or new experiences.

Use Your Practical Nature
You are good at seeing what is realistic. This can make you great at saving money, planning, or building things that last. Use this skill to help yourself and others.

Stay Balanced

Remember that too much of anything can lead to problems. It is great to be stable, but not if it means you never try anything new. Find a balance that works for you.

Moving Forward

Now that we have a clearer view of the bull symbol and the major traits linked with Taurus, we can look deeper into how these traits appear in other parts of life. Future chapters will talk about how Taurus behaves in friendships, family life, and the workplace. We will also see how a Taurus can handle money matters, build daily habits, and more.

By understanding the bull symbol, we begin to see why Taurus is considered an earth sign that values calm, comfort, and reliability. We also see how the stubborn and strong-willed side can show up. This background sets the stage for everything else we will discuss in the book.

CHAPTER 3: TAURUS IN ASTROLOGY BASICS

Astrology is a system that looks at the positions and movements of celestial bodies—like the sun, moon, and planets—and tries to connect those positions to patterns in human behavior and life events. When someone says they are a Taurus, they usually mean their sun sign is Taurus. This happens if the sun was in the part of the sky called Taurus at the time they were born. But there is more to astrology than just the sun sign. Astrology basics include understanding the birth chart, the planets, the houses, and the ways these parts can interact.

In this chapter, we will look at how astrology is organized, how Taurus fits into that bigger picture, and how different parts of a birth chart might affect someone's Taurus qualities. We will keep the discussion simple, so it is easy to follow.

The Zodiac Wheel and Sun Signs

The Zodiac Wheel
The zodiac is like a big circle in the sky, divided into twelve parts, each part named for a sign such as Taurus, Gemini, or Leo. Each sign covers about 30 degrees of that big circle, making the full 360-degree wheel. From an Earth point of view, the sun appears to move through these signs over the course of a year.

Sun Sign Basics
The sun sign is usually the most talked about part of astrology. If your birthday falls between about April 20 and May 20, you are often called a Taurus. People might check their sun sign horoscope and

see if it matches their current mood or events. The sun sign is about the core of someone's character, the main traits and motivations that guide them in life. In previous chapters, we touched on how Taurus is often described as steady, practical, and comfort-loving.

Why the Sun Sign is So Popular

One reason sun signs are the most popular part of astrology is that they are easy to figure out. All you need is your birthday. But keep in mind, astrology goes deeper. People interested in more complex details look beyond the sun sign at other planets, the moon, and even how the sky was arranged at the exact time of birth.

Beyond the Sun Sign

The Birth Chart

A birth chart is a map of where the sun, moon, and planets were located in the zodiac at the moment someone was born. It is made of twelve sections called houses. Each planet and sign combination might point to a specific area of life, such as emotions, communication, or relationships.

Moon Sign

The moon sign is said to represent inner feelings, emotional responses, and hidden desires. A person with a Taurus sun might have a moon sign in a different sign, which can add variety to their character. For example, a Taurus sun with a Leo moon might be more outgoing than a Taurus sun with a Pisces moon.

Rising Sign (Ascendant)

The rising sign, also called the ascendant, is the sign that was rising on the eastern horizon at the time of birth. It is sometimes described as the "mask" people wear, showing how they appear to others, especially in new situations. A Taurus sun might have a rising sign that changes how they first come across. For instance, if the rising sign is Libra, they might appear more social or charming upon first meeting, compared to a Taurus sun with a Scorpio rising, who might seem more private.

Other Planets

Each planet in a chart has a role. Mercury is about communication, Venus is about attraction and comfort, Mars is about action, Jupiter about growth, Saturn about discipline, and so on. If Taurus appears in different spots of someone's birth chart (like Mercury in Taurus or Mars in Taurus), they could show Taurus-like qualities in those parts of life.

For someone who is a Taurus sun, noticing where other planets are can explain why they might not fit the usual Taurus stereotype perfectly. They may have plenty of planets in fire or air signs, making them more energetic or talkative.

The Importance of Taurus as a Fixed Sign

Besides being an earth sign, Taurus is also known as a fixed sign. There are three types of signs in astrology: cardinal, fixed, and mutable. Each type has a different way of handling change and motion.

Cardinal Signs

Aries, Cancer, Libra, and Capricorn are called cardinal signs. These signs are seen as initiators. They like to start new projects or take the first step.

Fixed Signs

Taurus, Leo, Scorpio, and Aquarius are the fixed signs. They are associated with persistence and steadiness. Once they set their mind on something, they follow through. They often have clear determination.

Mutable Signs
Gemini, Virgo, Sagittarius, and Pisces are the mutable signs. These signs are said to be flexible and open to adapting.

Since Taurus is a fixed sign, it is linked with steadiness and reliability. People who are Taurus might remain committed to their goals. Once they decide on a plan, they keep going forward. This is part of why Taurus is considered patient and consistent.

Taurus Through the Twelve Houses

In a birth chart, each of the twelve houses stands for a different part of life. Here is a simple look at how Taurus might feel in each house, though the real effect depends on which planet is in that house along with Taurus.

First House: The First House is about self-identity and how others see you. Taurus here might show someone who appears calm, practical, and patient right from the moment people meet them.

Second House: The Second House deals with resources, money, and personal values. Taurus in the Second House fits well, as Taurus is linked with security and comfort. This might mean a natural skill in handling money or seeking financial stability.

Third House: The Third House is about communication and local environment (like siblings, neighbors, and small daily interactions). Taurus in the Third House might communicate in a calm, steady way. They might like learning through hands-on experiences.

Fourth House: The Fourth House is about home and family life. Taurus in this house might enjoy a cozy, stable home. They could be the kind of person who loves to keep the household routine steady, with a focus on comfort.

Fifth House: The Fifth House is about hobbies, creativity, and fun activities. Taurus here might enjoy hobbies that involve the senses, like cooking, painting, or music. They might be methodical but also appreciate pleasant experiences.

Sixth House: The Sixth House deals with daily work, routines, and health. Taurus here might have a consistent approach to health habits, or might like to follow a regular daily schedule at work. They could be reliable coworkers who prefer a predictable work environment.

Seventh House: The Seventh House is about partnerships and one-on-one connections. Taurus here might seek a loyal partner who values security. They may be steady in relationships and take their time before committing.

Eighth House: The Eighth House deals with deep changes, shared resources, and personal growth through challenges. Taurus here might resist big changes at first, but once they adapt, they might handle their shared finances or emotional bonds with care.

Ninth House: The Ninth House is about learning, beliefs, and exploring the broader world. Taurus here might approach learning in a realistic and step-by-step manner. They may prefer to study topics that have practical use.

Tenth House: The Tenth House is linked with career and public image. Taurus here might have a reputation for being dependable and stable in their line of work. They might aim for long-term security in their career.

Eleventh House: The Eleventh House is about groups, friendships, and hopes for the future. Taurus here might bring a calm energy to group projects. They often make steady contributions and might focus on practical goals that benefit the group.

Twelfth House: The Twelfth House is about hidden matters, solitude, and the unconscious mind. Taurus here might find comfort in quiet time alone, perhaps working on practical tasks that help them feel grounded. They may have a gentle way of dealing with private emotions.

These descriptions are very general. A full reading involves looking at which planets are in these houses, the angles between planets, and more.

Taurus and Planetary Aspects

In astrology, aspects are the angles between planets in a chart. They can show if the planets are helping each other or causing tension. If Taurus is strong in a chart (for example, a Taurus sun or several planets in Taurus), the aspects it makes with other signs can change how Taurus qualities show up.

- **Trine (120 degrees)**: This is usually considered a smooth aspect. If Taurus forms a trine with another earth sign like Virgo or Capricorn, the person might be very practical, grounded, and steady.

- **Square (90 degrees)**: This can bring tension. If Taurus squares a sign like Leo or Aquarius, the person might feel conflicts between wanting stability and wanting freedom or recognition.

- **Opposition (180 degrees)**: Taurus is opposite Scorpio in the zodiac. This can create a balance or a tug-of-war between security (Taurus) and transformation (Scorpio).

Understanding these aspects can give more clues about how Taurus energy might work in someone's life. Someone with many supportive aspects to their Taurus sun might feel more balanced, while someone with more difficult aspects might feel tension and learn to adapt to it over time.

The Role of the North Node and South Node

The North Node and South Node are points in the chart linked with personal growth (North Node) and habits or comfort zones (South Node). They are not planets, but many who study astrology believe they offer guidance about life direction.

- **North Node in Taurus**: Some might say this points to lessons about stability, patience, and learning to enjoy the present moment. A person with this placement might be encouraged to develop Taurus-like qualities.

- **South Node in Taurus**: This could mean the person is already used to Taurus traits and might lean on them too much. They might need to stretch themselves by exploring qualities of the opposite sign, Scorpio, such as learning to handle deeper changes.

These ideas about the Nodes show one of many ways astrology tries to highlight themes in a person's life.

How People Use Taurus Astrology Basics in Real Life

Self-Awareness
By looking at where Taurus sits in their birth chart, a person might learn more about their approach to specific areas of life. This can help them decide if they want to keep strengthening those Taurus traits or try to balance them with other qualities.

Setting Goals

Knowing that Taurus is steady and careful, some people set goals that match that energy. They might break big tasks into smaller steps, working slowly but surely toward their aim. This matches Taurus's calm approach and avoids rushing.

Relationships and Communication

People who are close to a Taurus might learn that Taurus folks prefer clear, practical conversations. This can help reduce misunderstandings. Also, friends and partners of a Taurus might expect them to resist sudden decisions. Being patient with a Taurus can help them feel more open to the idea of trying something new.

Work and Career

A strong Taurus presence in a birth chart might guide a person toward careers where stability or practicality is important. This could be anything from agriculture to banking, art, design, or anything that involves building or crafting. They often look for long-term security in whatever they do.

Common Questions About Taurus in Astrology

"Why do some Taurus people seem so different from each other?"
This can happen because each person's birth chart is unique. Even if two people share a Taurus sun, they might have different moon signs, rising signs, or other planet placements that shape their personalities.

"Does my Taurus sun mean I will have a certain kind of life?"
Astrology is not meant to be a strict rulebook. It is a way to notice patterns. People still have free will, and their environment and choices also affect what happens in life.

"Do all Taurus people dislike change?"
 Many Taurus individuals are slow to accept big changes, but this does not mean they never change. Some might actually enjoy change if it is on their own terms and if they can see a practical reason for it.

"Is Taurus only important if it is my sun sign?"
 No. Taurus can be important in different ways if it appears in other parts of the birth chart. For example, if someone's moon is in Taurus, they might feel calm when surrounded by comfort or nature. If someone's Mercury is in Taurus, they might speak in a slow and thoughtful way.

Taurus and the Concept of Timing

Astrology also deals with transits, which are the current positions of planets in the sky. At certain times, planets will pass through Taurus. For example, when the sun moves into Taurus each year around April 20, it is "Taurus season," and some might feel an increased focus on Taurus themes like security and patience. Other planets, like Mercury or Venus, might also spend time in Taurus, affecting communication style or sense of attraction during those periods.

People who have a lot of Taurus placements in their birth chart might notice these times more strongly. They might feel more motivated to focus on practical projects, or they might feel a bit uneasy if they do not enjoy the routine that is happening. Every person can react differently, and astrology suggests that having awareness of these transits can help someone make the most of that energy.

Misconceptions About Taurus in Astrology

"Taurus is only about relaxation or laziness."
 This is not accurate. While Taurus does enjoy calm and can move at a slow pace, it can also be very hard-working. Once Taurus

individuals decide on a goal, they can be quite determined, working steadily until they reach it.

"Taurus is not interested in deeper or complex ideas."
Actually, Taurus can be very thoughtful. They simply prefer to see if an idea can work in real life. They might not talk in circles about a theory but will try to see a realistic angle.

"Taurus cannot adapt to anything new."
Taurus might not like sudden changes, but they can adapt if given enough time. Once they see a clear benefit or get a chance to prepare, Taurus can handle shifts in routine.

Why Study Taurus in Astrology?

Some people see astrology as a tool for self-discovery. By studying Taurus, they might realize they do love peaceful environments, they do prefer consistency, and they do sometimes struggle with being too stubborn. This can be a first step toward understanding themselves better. Others might look at Taurus if they have a partner, friend, or child who is a Taurus, wanting to learn how to encourage them. A teacher might notice a Taurus student who works best with clear instructions and a calm classroom.

In the end, astrology is one way among many to see patterns in people's behavior. Not everyone believes in it, and that is okay. Those who do find meaning in it often say that learning about their sign helps them see why they act and feel the way they do. Taurus, with its focus on security, calm, and steady growth, can bring an interesting perspective to many parts of life.

CHAPTER 4: TAURUS ELEMENT AND PLANET

In astrology, each sign is connected to an element (fire, earth, air, or water) and a ruling planet that is said to give certain qualities to that sign. For Taurus, the element is Earth, and the ruling planet is Venus. This pairing helps show why Taurus is often described as grounded, steady, and drawn to comfort. In this chapter, we will explore the role of the Earth element, what it means for Taurus, and how Venus, as the ruling planet, influences the way Taurus might feel about relationships, beauty, and resources.

The Four Elements in Astrology

Astrology groups the twelve signs into four elements:

1. **Fire (Aries, Leo, Sagittarius)**: Often linked with passion, creativity, and strong impulses.

2. **Earth (Taurus, Virgo, Capricorn)**: Often linked with practicality, patience, and staying grounded.

3. **Air (Gemini, Libra, Aquarius)**: Often linked with thinking, communication, and social interactions.

4. **Water (Cancer, Scorpio, Pisces)**: Often linked with emotions, intuition, and empathy.

Because Taurus is an Earth sign, it leans toward a more physical, tangible, and steady approach to life.

Earth Element and Taurus

Grounded Nature
Earth signs are said to be close to the physical world. They appreciate real things they can feel, see, taste, or smell. Taurus in particular might love pleasant textures, good food, or soothing music. This ties back to the idea that Taurus values comfort.

Practical Problem-Solving
People with a strong Earth element often look for solutions that make sense in everyday life. They might not get lost in theories. Taurus is known for thinking about whether something can be done realistically before acting. This makes Taurus good at tasks that need focus and patience.

Steady Progress
Earth signs usually prefer to build things slowly. Taurus is no different. If a Taurus wants to improve at a skill, they might practice over time. This can help them master tasks, especially those that need consistent effort. They might not always jump at new ideas, but once they commit, they do their best.

Resistance to Change
The Earth element can sometimes be stubborn. Because Taurus is an Earth sign, it might resist sudden changes. It prefers stable ground under its feet. This can be a strength in times of chaos, but it can also make it hard for Taurus to adapt when quick shifts are necessary.

Balancing Earth with Other Elements

Even though Taurus is an Earth sign, people are not just one element. Their birth chart might have planets in fire, air, or water signs. For instance, a Taurus sun with a moon in a water sign like Pisces might be more emotional than a typical Taurus.

- **Earth and Fire**: This can bring warmth and excitement to the steady Earth. It might make a Taurus more willing to try new things.

- **Earth and Air**: This can bring bright ideas and clear thinking, helping Taurus become more flexible in discussions.

- **Earth and Water**: This can bring deeper emotional awareness, making Taurus more caring and empathetic.

When these elements mix, it creates a more unique personality. Still, at the core, Taurus keeps its Earth-based focus on reality and tangibility.

Venus, the Ruling Planet of Taurus

Venus in Astrology
Venus is named after the Roman goddess of love and beauty. In astrology, it is connected with the ways people form relationships, their sense of harmony, and what they find attractive.

What It Means to Be Ruled by Venus
If a sign is ruled by a planet, that planet is said to have a strong effect on the sign's traits. Because Venus rules Taurus, many Taurus individuals are believed to have a natural sense for beauty and comfort. They might be good at creating pleasant surroundings, whether that is by decorating their home or hosting a calm gathering with friends.

Venus and Love
Venus is linked closely with love and affection. For Taurus, this can mean loyalty in relationships and a desire to form strong bonds. Taurus might take relationships seriously, preferring long-lasting connections over brief ones. They might show love through

thoughtful gestures and a willingness to share comfort with a partner or friend.

Venus and Material Resources
Venus also has a side that deals with money and possessions. This is because the ancient idea of beauty also includes things that make life easier or more enjoyable. Taurus, being ruled by Venus, might put importance on saving or earning enough money to feel secure and content. They could see money as a way to maintain a cozy, comfortable life.

The Dual Influence of Earth and Venus

The combination of Earth as an element and Venus as a ruler shapes Taurus in distinct ways:

Love of Sensory Delights
Earth makes Taurus grounded, while Venus encourages them to enjoy pleasant experiences. This can mean delight in good food, a soft blanket, or a beautiful piece of music.

Patience in Relationships
The Earth element's patient approach, combined with Venus's focus on harmony, can lead Taurus to give their relationships a lot of care. They might not rush into anything romantic but will take time to make sure they trust a person.

Desire for Stability
Taurus can be known for wanting a solid home base. The Earth side likes stability, and Venus wants a comfortable setting. So, a Taurus might take extra steps to make sure they have enough resources to feel at ease.

Artistic Flair

While Taurus may not be as flashy as a fire sign, it can still have a quiet artistic sense. Because of Venus, Taurus might enjoy painting, music, design, or anything that involves creating beauty in a practical way.

How Taurus Expresses Venus Energy

Showing Affection

Taurus might show care by giving a comforting hug or planning a nice meal. They might also show affection by providing practical support, like helping fix something around the house.

Seeking Harmony

Taurus often avoids needless conflict. Though they can stand up for themselves if they must, they generally prefer peaceful interactions. Venus's influence can make them dislike loud arguments or tension in their environment.

Creating Welcoming Spaces

Because Venus is about aesthetics, many Taurus individuals have an eye for what looks or feels good. They might pick soft colors, arrange furniture in a pleasing way, or keep their space clean and organized.

Understanding Taurus' Connection to Venus Compared to Libra

Venus also rules Libra, but these two signs differ in how they show Venus energy.

- **Taurus (Earth Sign, Fixed)**: Shows Venus energy through a calm, hands-on approach. Prefers to build stable attachments and appreciates tangible comfort.

- **Libra (Air Sign, Cardinal)**: Shows Venus energy through social interaction, fairness, and balance in relationships. Focuses more on ideas of harmony and cooperation.

This difference highlights how the same planet can manifest in unique ways, depending on the element and the mode (fixed or cardinal) of each sign.

Venus Transits Through Taurus

Sometimes, Venus will move through Taurus in the current sky. When this happens, people might feel a collective focus on the Taurus side of Venus. This can mean:

- **Desire for Comfort**: Many might want to spend more time at home, enjoy nice foods, or appreciate beauty in simple things.

- **Increased Creativity**: Some people might feel inspired to do projects linked to art or design.

- **Focus on Relationships**: People might feel an urge to strengthen connections or seek calm in their partnerships.

Taurus individuals might feel this transit more strongly because it highlights their sign's ruler. They could feel more confident, more relaxed, or more enthusiastic about their personal interests during that time.

Challenges Linked to Earth and Venus for Taurus

No element or ruling planet is without its challenges. Taurus might face some of these hurdles:

Overattachment to Comfort
Because Earth signs can be cautious and Venus can love ease, a Taurus might cling to routines or material items more than is helpful. They might hesitate to leave a comfortable situation, even if it is not helping them grow in a positive way.

Financial Overconcern
Since Venus relates to money and Taurus values stability, some Taurus individuals can become too worried about finances. They might spend too much or become overly focused on saving, depending on their personal habits. A balanced approach is helpful.

Slow to Open Up
Taurus might be so steady that it takes a long time to show emotions or try new things. While this caution can protect them from harm, it can also cause them to miss out on positive experiences.

Sensitivity to Discord
If an environment is tense, Taurus can feel uneasy. They value harmony, so arguments or disharmony can cause stress. This might make them avoid speaking up about important issues, fearing conflict.

Practical Advice for Balancing Earth and Venus Energies

Plan for Change
Because Earth signs can resist sudden changes, it helps for Taurus to plan in small steps. If they know a change is coming, they can prepare, both financially and emotionally. This reduces stress while allowing them to adapt.

Enjoy Beauty Wisely
Venus loves nice things, but it is smart for Taurus to keep a balanced approach. If they want to buy something, they might ask

themselves, "Is this a good use of resources? Will it really help me feel good, or is it just a temporary pleasure?"

Practice Emotional Openness
Sharing feelings in small doses can help Taurus become more comfortable expressing emotions. It may feel strange at first, but it can lead to better understanding with friends and loved ones.

Set Gentle Boundaries
Taurus does not like arguments, but it is still important to speak up if they need something. Setting kind but clear boundaries can help them maintain the peace they value.

Earth Element Activities That Suit Taurus

Because Taurus is an Earth sign, activities that involve the senses and nature often feel pleasing:

Gardening
Working with plants can be relaxing, allowing Taurus to connect with the soil and watch things grow. This practical hobby fits well with the Earth element.

Cooking or Baking
Creating meals allows Taurus to use their sense of taste and smell. They can try recipes that are not too complex but still feel comforting.

Crafting or Building
Anything involving the hands, like pottery, woodworking, or sewing, can be a good match for Taurus. They can see real results from their efforts, which is satisfying.

Outdoor Walks

Quiet time in a park or near a lake can help Taurus feel more connected to the earth. The simple act of observing nature can bring them peace and refresh their mind.

The Symbolic Side of Venus for Taurus

In ancient myths, Venus (or Aphrodite in Greek stories) was not just about romance but also about harmony in the natural world. Fields growing crops and people living happily were considered part of her domain. For Taurus, these themes of growth and comfort align with the Earth element. It is as though Venus's nurturing side meets Taurus's desire for real, stable foundations, forming a sign that is both caring and down-to-earth.

Comparing Taurus to Other Earth Signs

Taurus shares the Earth element with Virgo and Capricorn, but each has a distinct focus:

1. **Taurus**: Steady, comfort-loving, patient. Focuses on security and the senses.

2. **Virgo**: Detail-oriented, helpful, analytical. Focuses on solving problems in a systematic way.

3. **Capricorn**: Ambitious, disciplined, goal-driven. Focuses on achieving success over time.

All three Earth signs value practicality, but Taurus may be more relaxed than Capricorn or Virgo, seeking a slow and peaceful route to achieving its aims.

Venus's Influence in Day-to-Day Interactions

A Taurus might show Venus energy in small ways:

- **Small Gestures of Kindness**: They might bring you a snack, fix a broken item, or offer a cozy spot to rest.

- **Eye for Beauty**: They might notice details like a lovely flower arrangement or an interesting fabric pattern.

- **Steady Comforting Presence**: Taurus might not give long pep talks, but they can sit quietly with someone, offering calm support.

These day-to-day expressions can help others feel relaxed and secure around a Taurus.

Deeper Emotional Side

While Taurus is often described as calm or even reserved, the influence of Venus suggests there can be a deeper emotional depth, especially when they feel safe. They might enjoy sharing life's simpler joys with people they trust. Once they open up, a Taurus can be quite affectionate and devoted, though they might still need a sense of predictability in the relationship.

Final Thoughts on Taurus's Earth Element and Venus

Taurus stands out as a sign that blends Earth's steady energy with Venus's focus on warmth and harmony. This unique blend can make Taurus people dependable friends, thoughtful partners, and reliable workers. At the same time, it can make them very determined to hold onto what feels safe and comfortable.

For those who are Taurus, knowing about these influences can help them see why they might crave certain routines or why they take pleasure in small comforts. For those who know and care about a Taurus, understanding the Earth element and Venus can provide insight into how to share meaningful experiences with them—perhaps by offering a stable home life, a nurturing friendship, or a supportive environment at work.

Tips for Appreciating Taurus Energy

Encourage Their Love of Beauty
If you have a Taurus in your life, you can plan simple activities like visiting a local garden or trying a new recipe. These experiences let them enjoy the senses without forcing them out of their comfort zone too quickly.

Give Them Time to Adjust
Taurus might need extra moments to accept changes. Being patient with them can help them feel less pressured.

Respect Their Need for Stability
Taurus might plan for the future carefully. Instead of rushing them, try to see how their slow-and-steady method can lead to solid results.

Offer Kind Touch
Since Taurus can appreciate physical comfort, a gentle hug or a pat on the shoulder (if they are okay with it) can mean a lot.

CHAPTER 5: STRENGTHS OF TAURUS

When people talk about a zodiac sign, they often mention qualities or traits that are considered strong points. For Taurus, these strong points go beyond simple words like "patient" or "reliable." They become visible in many parts of life, whether it is in long-term friendships, family roles, tasks at work, or personal interests. In this chapter, we will look at the key strengths that are often linked with Taurus and see how these strengths can shine in different situations. While every person is unique, a Taurus might find these qualities easier to display or develop because of the nature of their sign.

What Are Strengths?

Strengths are qualities that help people do well. They are not the same as talents, which are special abilities that can come naturally to a person. Strengths are more like helpful traits that can be practiced or shown in many tasks. For example, a Taurus might have a calm attitude that allows them to stay steady under stress, and this calmness is a strength because it can help them handle problems more easily.

We should remember that a trait is only a strength if it is used in a positive way. For instance, patience is helpful when dealing with a difficult problem, but if someone takes patience to an extreme, they might miss important deadlines. So, the strengths of Taurus are best used in balance. Once a Taurus understands how to keep that balance, they can get a lot of benefits from these qualities.

Steadiness and Consistency

One of the most notable strengths that people connect with Taurus is steadiness. This word means that a Taurus can keep the same level of effort and focus over time. They do not start projects with a big rush only to stop halfway; instead, they maintain a calm, regular pace. This can be an advantage in many areas of life, such as:

Schoolwork or Studies: A Taurus might set aside a certain amount of time each day to work on homework, slowly making progress until they complete it. They might not do all of it in one night, but by the end of the week, they have handled their tasks carefully.

Hobbies and Projects: If a Taurus takes up a hobby, they might practice it regularly. They do not feel the need to be the best right away, but they trust that steady effort will help them improve over time.

Long-Term Goals: Some goals require patience, like learning a musical instrument or mastering a new language. Taurus folks can remain consistent, practicing a little each day and seeing gradual improvement.

The power of consistency is that it often leads to stable results. If someone does something at a slow but regular pace, they are less likely to burn out. This approach can make Taurus a strong presence in any group or team, providing a sense of reassurance that everything will be done as promised.

Reliability and Trustworthiness

Close to the idea of steadiness is the strength of reliability. A reliable person is someone you can count on. If a Taurus friend says they will help you with a project, you can expect them to show up on time and do what they agreed to do. This level of trustworthiness can make Taurus a valued part of many social circles. In fact, many people turn to Taurus individuals when they need someone they know will be there no matter what.

Being reliable does not simply mean doing tasks. It also means being consistent with words and actions. A Taurus might:

Keep Private Information Safe: They often do not rush to share secrets or personal details about others. This helps them earn trust in friendships.

Offer a Steady Opinion: Even if others are unsure, a Taurus might give a clear and measured point of view. This can help a team or group decide how to move forward.

Support Loved Ones Over Time: Instead of giving help only once, a Taurus might continue checking on a friend, making sure everything is okay. This long-term caring can be a great source of comfort.

Reliability may not be the most attention-grabbing quality, but it is one of the most valuable. Friends, family, and coworkers often appreciate having someone around who keeps their word and follows through.

Patience in Challenging Situations

Patience is another key strength of Taurus. This goes hand in hand with steadiness, but it focuses more on the way Taurus deals with problems or delays. For example, if something unexpected happens, like a problem at work or school, a Taurus might not panic. They might take a deep breath, think about the steps they need to take, and then handle each step calmly.

In everyday life, this patience can appear in many ways:

Waiting for Outcomes: If a Taurus applies for a job or a new school, they might handle the waiting period more calmly than some other signs. They recognize that certain things simply take time.

Dealing with Problems: When something breaks at home, a Taurus might not rush into fixing it without thinking. Instead, they carefully look at the issue, gather the right tools, and then begin.

Managing Emotions: While everyone can feel upset sometimes, a Taurus might hold onto a calmer front for a longer time. This does not mean they do not get upset; they just might have more practice waiting before reacting.

Patience does not imply ignoring problems. Rather, it means a Taurus might handle them in a slow, careful way instead of rushing around in panic. This approach can help prevent mistakes that come from making choices too quickly.

Practical Thinking and Problem-Solving

Taurus is often seen as a sign that likes real, hands-on solutions. When a challenge appears, a Taurus might look for the most direct and realistic way to solve it. They might not be the type to come up with wild ideas. Instead, they want to see which approach is the most likely to work in the real world.

This practical thinking can help with:

Everyday Decisions: What is the best way to budget money? Which tools are needed for a home project? Taurus tends to pick wise options that help them avoid wasting time or resources.

Plans and Goals: If a Taurus decides they want to learn a new skill, they may break down the steps, gather the supplies, and follow a clear schedule.

Helping Others: Friends might ask a Taurus for advice when they need an approach that is grounded in reality. A Taurus can help pick the best route forward based on facts and logic.

Practical thinking may not sound as exciting as being very creative or spontaneous. But many times, the ability to see what is realistic and useful is a major strength. It can save time, reduce stress, and lead to solutions that stand the test of time.

Strong Sense of Responsibility

Taurus often feels a strong sense of responsibility. This does not just refer to big tasks, like taking care of a family or leading a group project. It can also appear in smaller ways, like always remembering to feed a pet at the same time each day or making sure they finish what they start.

A sense of responsibility can help in many parts of life:

Work and Career: Employers often look for workers who take their duties seriously. A Taurus might show up on time, follow workplace rules, and keep projects running smoothly.

Home and Family: A Taurus might be the family member who organizes monthly bills or keeps a schedule for chores, ensuring that nothing is forgotten.

Personal Commitments: If a Taurus joins a club or a group, they will likely do their best not to let anyone down. If they make a promise, they treat it as important.

This responsibility ties back to the idea of trustworthiness. By handling their tasks carefully, Taurus individuals build a solid reputation. People around them learn that they can depend on the Taurus to keep things going as planned.

Calm Under Pressure

In many situations, stress can cause people to act hurried or become anxious. One of Taurus's great strengths is staying calm under pressure. While everyone can feel stress, Taurus might manage it by returning to what is familiar or steady. They might hold onto routines that soothe them—like listening to calming music or sticking to a simple daily plan—to keep their nerves in check.

Being calm under pressure helps in:

Conflict Situations: If friends or coworkers are arguing, a Taurus might step in, speak quietly, and try to bring everyone back to a more relaxed state.

Unexpected Changes: Even though Taurus prefers stability, when a change does happen, they might tackle it slowly rather than exploding with strong emotions.

High-Stakes Events: Whether it is taking a test or giving a presentation, Taurus might handle these moments by focusing on what they can control, such as preparing well and double-checking their materials.

This calm outlook also gives Taurus individuals time to think. Instead of being driven by panic, they can often make more thoughtful choices, even when things get tough.

Quiet Determination

Some might say that Taurus is stubborn, but a more positive way to see this is "quiet determination." When a Taurus decides on a goal, they keep going until they reach it. They may not shout about it or boast, but they keep working behind the scenes, taking small, steady steps. Over time, these steps can lead to a big achievement.

Examples of quiet determination might include:

- **Learning Skills Over Time:** A Taurus might learn to play a musical instrument, practice sports, or gain expertise in a craft by putting in hours of practice week after week.

- **Saving Resources:** If they want to save money for something important, they might slowly put aside funds, skipping small luxuries to reach their bigger goal.

- **Personal Challenges:** If a Taurus faces a health or fitness challenge, they might develop a plan and stick to it, day after day, until they see results.

This strong determination can be a powerful advantage. It allows Taurus individuals to handle long tasks that other people might give up on.

Loyalty and Devotion

Loyalty is often described as a key strength of Taurus. They can be very devoted to friends, family, and partners, offering support that lasts. When a Taurus bonds with someone, they usually give that person respect, kindness, and love for a long time. They are not likely to drift away easily.

Being loyal does not mean that a Taurus will always agree with everything a loved one does, but it means they will stand by that person through both good and bad. Loyalty can also appear in the way Taurus people guard the secrets or interests of someone they care about. They are often unwilling to break that trust.

This loyalty can be a great strength because it helps form stable relationships. Friends and family know they can count on a Taurus for help, sympathy, or just a steady presence. That bond can become a source of comfort and safety, which is important in a changing world.

Appreciation for the Senses

Taurus has a connection to what people sometimes call "the senses." This means they often notice details in sounds, smells, tastes, or textures that other signs might miss. While this might seem like a small detail, it can actually be a strength. When a Taurus can fully appreciate their surroundings, they might also create enjoyable and cozy environments for themselves and others.

A few ways this can be a strength:

- **Hosting and Hospitality:** Taurus individuals might pay attention to details such as comfortable seating, gentle lighting, or pleasing music when hosting visitors, making people feel at ease.

- **Creative Hobbies:** Some Taurus folks who enjoy art, cooking, or other creative tasks can use their strong awareness of color, flavor, or texture to produce something delightful.

- **Self-Care:** A Taurus might find ways to relax at home through scented candles, soft blankets, or calming music. This can help them rest well and stay healthy.

In a fast-paced world, the ability to slow down and appreciate small things is valuable. It can lead to less stress and a happier outlook.

Self-Motivation and Personal Discipline

Another area where Taurus can show strength is self-motivation. Because they are steady and determined, Taurus individuals might not need someone else to constantly remind them to do their chores or meet a goal. They can often motivate themselves. This also involves personal discipline, which means sticking to a plan or a rule they set for themselves.

For example, if a Taurus decides they want to exercise a certain number of times a week, they might mark it on their calendar and follow that plan, even if they do not always feel like it. This level of personal discipline can help them accomplish what they want in life.

Sometimes, it also means knowing when to stop or slow down. A Taurus might tell themselves, "I will go to bed by 10 p.m. so I am rested," and then actually follow that rule. While this might sound simple, it can be challenging for many people. Taurus's sense of self-discipline is a real advantage.

Observing Patterns and Details

Being practical and connected to the real world means that Taurus individuals can be good at noticing patterns or details that others might miss. They might see how a small change in a routine could lead to an improvement, or they might catch mistakes in a plan. Because of this, they can be helpful in roles that involve checking details, planning, or keeping things in order.

This skill might appear in:

- **Group Projects:** Taurus might spot a missing piece of information or point out a logical gap in a plan.

- **Artistic Work:** Whether they are painting or knitting, they might see small imperfections and correct them before they become bigger issues.

- **Personal Life:** A Taurus might notice that certain habits make them feel better or worse, and they can adjust accordingly.

This careful observation is a strength because it can prevent bigger problems and often makes projects turn out better. It also helps Taurus figure out the most practical steps to move forward.

Stability in Relationships and Groups

When people gather in a team or family setting, it can be helpful to have someone who brings a sense of calm and stability. Taurus often provides exactly that. They might not speak the loudest or take over the conversation, but they can offer a steady hand, making sure everyone feels safe and understood.

Taurus people might help groups by:

- **Being a Reliable Planner:** In a group of friends planning a simple event, Taurus might remember important details, such as the time, place, and what items are needed, ensuring that nothing is forgotten.
- **Calming Tension:** If two people in the group disagree, Taurus might speak in a calm voice or give each side a chance to share their view.

- **Offering Consistent Input:** They might not flip their opinion suddenly. Instead, they stick to their perspective, which can be reassuring when people are unsure about what to do.

This type of stability helps keep a group functioning in a less chaotic way. When the group knows there is at least one person who will remain level-headed, they can find common ground more easily.

Long-Term Planning

Because Taurus is patient and practical, another strength is the ability to make plans that stretch over weeks, months, or even years. They do not always need instant results. If they decide on a major life goal—such as saving for something important, finishing an academic program, or building a skill—they can take small steps, one after another, until they succeed.

This long-term planning can appear in:

- **Financial Management:** Taurus might set aside a set amount of money each month, gradually building up savings to reach a larger objective.

- **Learning and Development:** Whether it is reading books or practicing a craft, Taurus can schedule time and keep going, even when the payoff is far in the future.

- **Career Paths:** A Taurus might start in a beginner-level job and stay with a company, slowly moving up because they keep meeting their goals.

This trait can bring a sense of security. Taurus people often trust that their steady work will pay off eventually, so they do not feel rushed to see quick results.

Balanced Temperament with Emotions

Even though Taurus does feel strong emotions at times, many Taurus individuals can keep a balanced temperament. This does not mean hiding feelings, but rather dealing with them in a calm manner. They might take time alone to think about a situation before responding, which can reduce regretful words or actions.

Examples of balanced temperament:

Discussions Rather Than Yelling: If a Taurus disagrees with someone, they might try to talk it out instead of getting loud or angry.

Seeking Practical Solutions: When upset, they look for ways to fix the problem rather than only focusing on how they feel. This can lead to more positive outcomes.

Respecting Personal Limits: If a Taurus feels overwhelmed, they might step back and rest instead of pushing themselves until they collapse.

By handling emotions in a measured way, Taurus can maintain good relationships and a calmer daily life.

Learning from Mistakes Gradually

Some people learn best by quick bursts of change, but Taurus often prefers a slower process. When they make mistakes, they might reflect on what happened and adjust step by step. This can be an advantage because it means they are less likely to repeat the same mistake if they have time to think about what went wrong.

They might do this by:

Keeping Notes or Records: Writing down what happened can help them see where the error occurred and what they can do differently next time.

Asking for Guidance: Taurus might seek out someone more experienced, but not in a rushed way. They will gather advice, analyze it, and then apply it in a practical manner.

Trying Small Adjustments: Instead of making big, sudden changes, they might test a small new approach and see if it fixes the problem.

This slow, careful way of learning can lead to steady progress over time. It also helps Taurus avoid making new problems in their rush to fix the old ones.

Inner Strength and Resilience

While Taurus is not always flashy, there is a quiet inner strength that many Taurus individuals possess. They can get through hard times by relying on their steadiness and determination. Even if they feel discouraged, they have a strong sense of self that keeps them moving. They might not talk about it loudly, but they keep going.

Some signs of Taurus resilience include:

Overcoming Personal Challenges: If they face a setback—like not getting the job they wanted—they might regroup, revise their resume, and apply again without losing hope.

Enduring Difficult Emotions: They might not instantly recover from sadness or anger, but they keep functioning and doing what needs to be done. Over time, they heal.

Supporting Others While Facing Their Own Problems: A Taurus might still lend a hand to friends even when they are going through a tough period themselves, showing quiet bravery.

This resilience is a great strength because it allows Taurus to bounce back from hardships while still offering stability to those around them.

Bringing Out the Best in These Strengths

Having these strengths does not mean they show up automatically. Often, a Taurus needs to recognize and practice them. Here are a few ways a Taurus can make sure they are using their strengths:

Set Clear Goals: Taurus can aim their steadiness and determination at something specific, whether it is a personal aim or a shared plan with others.

Stay Open to Feedback: Even though they like to solve problems on their own, listening to others can help them use their strengths more effectively.

Keep Track of Progress: By noting small achievements, Taurus can see how far they have come, which encourages them to keep going.

Relax with Purpose: Since Taurus likes comfort, making time for calm activities can recharge them so they can keep using their strengths in everyday life.

Potential Pitfalls of Strengths

Sometimes, strengths can become too strong and turn into challenges if not balanced. For example, patience is good, but too much patience might cause missed opportunities. Reliability is helpful, but if a Taurus takes on too many promises, they might end up overloaded. Here are a few reminders:

- **Balance Patience with Action:** Know when to move quickly if a situation calls for it.

- **Balance Practical Thinking with Openness:** Being realistic is great, but new or unusual ideas should not always be dismissed.

- **Balance Loyalty with Self-Care:** Being devoted to loved ones is kind, but make sure you also take care of your own needs.

Acknowledging these pitfalls can help a Taurus keep their strengths in the healthy range.

CHAPTER 6: WEAKNESSES OF TAURUS

While Taurus is known for many good qualities, no sign is without its challenges. Strengths and weaknesses often go together. What makes Taurus reliable and calm can also lead to certain problems, such as being overly stubborn or resisting necessary changes. In this chapter, we will focus on the more difficult traits or tendencies linked with Taurus and consider ways to address them. Remember, having these weaknesses does not mean a Taurus is doomed to fail. In fact, being aware of them is the first step toward improvement.

Why Look at Weaknesses?

It can be uncomfortable to look at the downsides of a personality, but understanding them can help a person grow. Weaknesses often arise from the same traits that form strengths. For example, being steady can turn into being stuck, and being loyal can turn into refusing to let go of something or someone harmful. By recognizing these traps, a Taurus can figure out how to adjust or find help from others.

Also, weaknesses do not make a person "bad." Everyone has areas that need more care. For Taurus, these areas might show up in specific situations or relationships. Once a Taurus knows what to watch for, they can learn methods to keep those less helpful behaviors under control.

Stubbornness and Resistance to Change

One of the most repeated critiques of Taurus is that they can be very stubborn. Stubbornness here means they hold onto opinions or habits, even when they are no longer helpful. This can show up in simple things, like refusing to change a daily routine, or in bigger life decisions, such as staying in a job they dislike rather than seeking new opportunities.

A few reasons for this trait include:

- **Comfort in Routine:** Taurus likes feeling safe in known patterns. Changing these patterns can feel risky, leading them to hold on to the old way.

- **Strong Beliefs:** Once a Taurus forms an opinion, they can find it hard to see another side. They might see changing that opinion as admitting defeat.

- **Fear of the Unknown:** Taurus might see the unknown as an unnecessary risk. Because they value stability, they avoid shaking things up.

How can Taurus handle stubbornness? One simple approach is to practice small changes regularly. For instance, if they always take the same route to work, they might try a different path once a week to show themselves that change does not have to be scary. They can also listen carefully to trusted friends who offer new ideas, making sure to weigh those ideas fairly.

Overattachment to Comfort

Taurus is linked with the search for security and ease. While this can be a good thing, it can also lead to staying "too comfortable."

Someone who is too comfortable might not push themselves to learn new skills or try new experiences. They might also spend a lot of time or money on small pleasures, risking their long-term goals.

Examples include:

- **Avoiding Challenges:** A Taurus might turn down a promotion because it involves learning new skills, deciding it is more comfortable to remain where they are.

- **Indulging in Luxury:** Because they appreciate nice things, some Taurus individuals might overspend on food, clothes, or entertainment, forgetting to save for more important goals.

- **Skipping Growth Opportunities:** Maybe a class or workshop could help them move forward, but they decide it is too much trouble to switch their routine.

To handle this, it helps to plan for growth in small steps. Taurus can keep some comforts while also setting aside time to gain new experiences. Trying something slightly different, like a new dish to cook or a nearby park to visit, can add just enough novelty to combat staying in one place.

Slowness to Act

While steadiness is a strength, it can also become slowness that causes missed chances. Because Taurus likes to make sure everything is lined up, they might take a long time to start. In a world that sometimes rewards quick action, this can be a disadvantage.

They might:

- **Delay Important Decisions:** A Taurus could spend weeks thinking about an offer, only to find that the opportunity has passed.

- **Wait for Perfect Conditions:** They may want everything to be just right before they move forward, which might never happen.

- **Lose Momentum in Projects:** If they do not keep a certain pace, they might get stuck and let a project fade away.

This does not mean Taurus should turn into someone who acts without thought. Instead, they can set deadlines for themselves, like, "I will make a choice by next Friday." They can also remind themselves that sometimes "good enough" is better than "perfect but never done."

Holding Onto Grudges

Loyalty is a great trait, but it can flip into its darker side: holding onto grudges. Because Taurus can be very devoted and has a strong sense of fairness, if they feel someone has betrayed them, they might not forgive easily. This can lead to conflicts that last much longer than they need to.

Signs of grudges include:

- **Avoiding Apologies:** Even if the other person admits wrongdoing, a Taurus might say, "That is not enough."

- **Storing Resentment:** They might remember small details of how someone hurt them, bringing it up again and again.

- **Building Walls:** A Taurus might cut off contact or emotional connection, even if the relationship could be saved through honest communication.

Letting go of grudges is not easy, but it can bring relief. Sometimes, speaking openly about how they feel can help a Taurus move forward. They might also benefit from writing down what happened, seeing if there is a solution that could help them forgive. Forgiving does not mean forgetting. It just means releasing the heavy burden of anger.

Overfocus on Material Security

Because Taurus is an earth sign connected with resources, they might care a lot about financial stability. While this can be positive, it can become a problem if Taurus becomes too focused on money or material items. They might measure their self-worth by how much they own or how secure their bank account is, ignoring other parts of life like friendships, emotional growth, and new interests.

Examples of overfocus might be:

- **Placing Money Above Relationships:** A Taurus might work so many hours to feel secure that they rarely spend time with family or friends.

- **Reluctance to Take Kind Risks:** They might not want to share or help a loved one because they worry it will jeopardize their own security.

- **Comparing Possessions:** A Taurus might feel anxious if they think they do not have as nice a car or home as someone else.

One idea to balance this is to remember that real security also involves healthy relationships and personal fulfillment. Taurus can still be wise with money but set limits on how much time or mental energy they devote to material concerns. They might try volunteering or spending time with loved ones, reminding themselves that not all value is measured in dollars.

Narrow Comfort Zone

Another weakness that can come from loving routine is having a very narrow comfort zone. Taurus might only like to do things a certain way and in a certain environment. Anything that does not fit this pattern can feel scary. This can limit their experiences, making them miss out on opportunities to learn about the world.

This can appear as:

- **Unwillingness to Travel Anywhere Different:** They might choose the same places to visit or the same restaurants each time.

- **Avoiding New People:** If Taurus only feels safe with people they have known for a long time, they might miss the chance to meet new friends or helpful contacts.

- **Sticking to Old Ways at Work:** They might resist new technology or methods even when they could make work easier.

Small steps can help expand their comfort zone. For example, Taurus can try joining a low-pressure social group or picking a simple new hobby. Over time, these actions can help them see that new experiences are not always threatening and can even be enjoyable.

Tendency to Be Possessive

Because Taurus is linked with security and a need for safety, sometimes this can become possessiveness. This is not always about material goods. It can also be about relationships. A Taurus might worry about losing something they care about—be it an object or a person—and they might act in ways that are too controlling.

Signs of possessiveness:

- **Checking Up on Friends or Partners Too Much:** They might feel uneasy if their loved one spends time with others, fearing it might lessen their bond.

- **Feeling Threatened by Sharing:** If they have a favorite item, they might hesitate to let even a trusted friend borrow it.

- **Arguments Over Loyalty:** A Taurus might demand constant reassurance from friends or partners that they are still important.

Reducing possessiveness involves trusting others and building self-confidence. If a Taurus trusts that people care about them, they will feel less need to control every situation. Sharing or lending small items can be a practical step to loosen the fear of losing property.

Getting Stuck in the Past

With a strong memory and an appreciation for what feels familiar, Taurus can hold onto the past—sometimes in a way that prevents them from moving forward. They might cling to old patterns, old possessions, or old hurts, finding it tough to make space for new possibilities.

This can show up as:

- **Keeping Old Items That Are No Longer Useful:** They might have trouble throwing away or donating things, even if they are not used anymore.

- **Continuing Old Arguments:** Similar to grudges, they might bring up past conflicts during new disagreements.

- **Missing the Present:** If their mind is focused on what once was, they may not notice chances that exist today.

Letting go of the past can involve gentle reminders that time moves on and that holding onto old situations can slow down present happiness. Taurus might find it helpful to do a regular cleanup, whether it is clearing old items or writing out old complaints to let them go.

Struggling with Quick Adaptation

While Taurus can eventually adjust to changes, they might struggle with situations that demand immediate shifts. This can be challenging in workplaces or life events where fast action is needed. Taurus might freeze up, hoping they will have more time to decide what to do.

A few examples:

- **Emergency Events:** If a problem arises that needs a solution right away, Taurus might feel overwhelmed because they cannot plan in their usual slow, steady way.

- **Sudden Plan Changes:** If the schedule changes last minute, Taurus might become irritated or anxious, feeling rushed.

- **Digital or Technological Updates:** If the phone or computer system is updated overnight, a Taurus might take a long time to adapt to the new features, feeling frustrated that the old system is gone.

To tackle this, Taurus can work on building "adaptation practice." They can simulate quick changes for fun, like a spontaneous day trip or a surprise meal choice, to prove to themselves they can handle unexpected things. Over time, this can lower the stress when real surprises happen.

Hidden Anger

While Taurus is often calm, that calm might hide anger that slowly builds over time. Because they try to avoid big blowups, they can store irritation until it becomes too big to hold in. At that point, they might have an outburst that surprises everyone around them.

This hidden anger might show itself as:

- **Passive-Aggressive Behaviors:** Instead of saying they are upset, Taurus might do small things like giving the silent treatment or making sarcastic comments.

- **Health Issues:** Bottling up anger can sometimes appear as headaches, stomach aches, or stress-related problems.

- **Huge Anger Episodes:** After a long period of calm, the anger might come out all at once in a very heated argument.

The best way to manage hidden anger is to express it in smaller, healthier steps. Talking to a trusted friend, writing thoughts in a journal, or calmly stating, "I am upset about this and need to talk," can prevent the anger from growing too large. It also helps Taurus maintain their calm nature without ignoring real feelings.

Being Overly Private

Some Taurus individuals prefer to keep their personal life to themselves. This can be good in some ways, protecting them from unwanted gossip or intrusion. However, it can also turn into a weakness if it keeps them from getting help or building close connections. In a group project, for instance, a Taurus might not share that they are struggling, leading them to fall behind without anyone knowing why.

This privacy can cause:

- **Isolation:** Others might think Taurus is uninterested in being close. This can lead to fewer meaningful friendships.

- **Missed Support:** If Taurus does not tell anyone about their challenges, they cannot receive advice or help.

- **Misunderstandings:** Friends or family might feel shut out and think Taurus does not trust them or care about them.

Balancing privacy with healthy sharing is important. Taurus can start by sharing small personal facts or asking for minor favors, then see that people's responses are often supportive, not judgmental.

Tendency to Overthink Practical Details

Taurus is practical, but sometimes they can get lost in small details and forget the big picture. They might spend a lot of time comparing prices before buying something minor, or they might postpone a decision because they want to check every tiny detail. In a fast-paced situation, this focus on details can slow them down or frustrate others.

This might look like:

- **Endless Research:** They research every type of product before making a purchase, even when the differences are slight.

- **Worrying Over Minor Flaws:** Taurus might not move forward with a project if they notice small imperfections, even if those flaws do not matter much in the long run.

- **Delaying Group Action:** If the group is ready to proceed, Taurus might say, "Wait, we have not looked at every option," causing the group to lose momentum.

One trick is to have a cutoff point. For instance, set a limit to how much research is done—like one hour or three websites. This ensures Taurus keeps their practical side but avoids getting stuck. They can also ask a friend or teammate to let them know when they have done enough checking.

Inflexibility in Group Settings

In group activities or team projects, Taurus might insist on doing things "their way" or might push back if someone suggests a new approach. This comes from the same part of their nature that likes consistency and comfort. But it can cause friction with others.

These problems might appear as:

- **Ignoring Others' Ideas:** A Taurus might act as though their plan is automatically better because they spent time thinking it through.

- **Refusal to Move from a Schedule:** If the group wants to change the schedule or rearrange duties, Taurus might be the one who says, "But we always do it like this."

- **Frustration with Different Work Styles:** If someone is more spontaneous, it can clash with Taurus's preference for slow, careful steps.

To address this, Taurus can practice compromise. Instead of insisting, they can try, "Let's combine your approach and mine. I will keep the schedule, but we can add your creative ideas." This builds a middle ground where everyone feels heard.

Hesitation to Try New Methods

Closely linked with resistance to change is the hesitation to try new methods, especially if the old method still works. Taurus might think, "Why fix something that is not broken?" While this logic can be sound, it might keep them from better or more modern ways of doing things.

This could mean:

- **Not Updating Skills:** In a technology-driven world, methods change fast. A Taurus might keep using outdated software or techniques until they are far behind.

- **Missing Efficiency:** New methods might save time or energy, but Taurus might not believe it until they see it proven many times.

- **Falling Behind Competitors:** If others adopt new ways while Taurus sticks to old habits, the Taurus individual might lose opportunities.

A balanced approach is to test a new method on a small scale. If it works, Taurus can adopt it more fully, feeling secure because they have seen the results first. This approach respects their need for caution but still opens the door to improvement.

Oversensitivity to Criticism

Though Taurus can appear tough on the outside, they can also be quite sensitive to criticism. Because they put care into what they do, they might take negative feedback personally. This can lead them to feel defensive or hurt instead of seeing how the feedback might help them improve.

They might react by:

- **Shutting Down:** A Taurus might stop listening entirely if they sense criticism is not coming from a friendly place.

- **Defending Without Reflecting:** They might argue back right away rather than asking questions to understand the critique better.

- **Holding a Grudge Against the Critic:** The Taurus might take it as a personal insult and never forget it.

To handle this, Taurus can try to remind themselves that not all criticism is an attack. Some of it can be helpful. It might help to ask clarifying questions: "Can you show me an example of what you mean?" or "How do you think I can improve?" By turning criticism into a conversation, Taurus might gain insights rather than just feeling hurt.

Risk of Boredom or Apathy

If Taurus stays in the same situation for too long without any challenge or excitement, they might start to feel bored or apathetic. This can lead them to go through the motions of daily life without much joy or curiosity, simply because they feel safe in that routine. Over time, this can reduce motivation.

Signs of boredom or apathy include:

- **Lack of Energy:** Taurus might do what they must but with very little enthusiasm.

- **Turning to Comforts Excessively:** They might watch the same shows, eat the same comfort foods, or stay in the same place instead of trying something new.

- **Avoiding New Interests:** If a friend suggests a new activity, they might shrug it off, saying they are not interested.

Breaking out of boredom does not require big gestures. Even small changes, like reading a different type of book or learning a short new skill, can refresh their daily life. Talking to friends who have different interests can also open windows to new activities.

Self-Doubt Hidden Behind Calm

Sometimes Taurus seems calm, but inside they can experience self-doubt, wondering if they are truly capable or deserving of success. This might stem from their careful approach: if they see others moving faster or taking bold steps, they could question if they are doing enough.

This doubt can:

- **Lead to Missed Opportunities:** They might not apply for a program or job because they worry they are not good enough.

- **Cause Quiet Stress:** Even if outwardly calm, they might be tense inside, worrying about failing.

- **Create a Need for Approval:** They might secretly want their friends or boss to tell them they are doing well, though they may not openly admit it.

Recognizing these feelings can help Taurus handle them. They can keep a record of their successes, reminding themselves of times they overcame doubt. They can also talk with supportive people who can offer encouragement without pushing them too far.

Handling Weaknesses in a Healthy Way

No one can remove all weaknesses from their personality, but they can manage them. For Taurus, this often means making small changes or practicing good habits that balance out their natural tendencies. Here are some practical tips:

Try Small Experiments: If Taurus tends to avoid new things, they can test out little changes—a new meal, a short visit to a different place, or a brief online course—to show themselves that variety can be safe and fun.

Set Time Limits: If Taurus gets stuck researching or worrying, they can say, "I will only spend one hour on this, and then I will act."

Work with Friends: If a Taurus does not like to adapt quickly, a friend who is more flexible might help them by suggesting a faster path. They can balance each other's styles.

Acknowledge Feelings: Taurus does not have to pretend they never get upset or worried. A simple, "I am feeling anxious about this change" can be the first step to handling it better.

Seek Professional Guidance: If stubbornness, anger, or possessiveness cause big problems, talking to a counselor or mentor can help a Taurus understand why they feel that way and how to adjust.

By using these tips, Taurus can keep their weaknesses from overwhelming them and even turn some challenges into learning moments.

CHAPTER 7: TAURUS IN FRIENDSHIPS

A friendship is often built on mutual trust, understanding, and shared activities. For Taurus, friendship can be a safe zone where they can show their calm and steady sides while also offering reliable support to those they care about. Like with all zodiac signs, each Taurus is different, but there are some common features that appear when Taurus people form and keep friendships. In this chapter, we will look at how Taurus typically acts with friends, what they look for in companions, and how they manage any bumps in the road. We will also look at the positive aspects that Taurus can bring to a friendship and some potential hurdles that might arise.

The Taurus Approach to Making Friends

When a Taurus meets new people, they usually do not rush to become close. They may appear friendly but careful, taking time to decide if they really connect with someone. This careful approach can be seen when they attend social events or join groups. Instead of standing in the center of the room or talking to everyone at once, they might stay in a smaller circle of people or chat with a few individuals quietly. This does not mean they dislike meeting others; they just need space to feel comfortable.

- **Observation First**: Taurus might watch how a person behaves, noticing if they are genuine and kind. They want to see if someone's actions match their words.

- **Small Steps**: They might start a conversation about simple topics—like favorite foods, music, or a recent show they watched—rather than jumping into deep, personal matters.

- **Testing the Waters**: Taurus could try small shared experiences with a new acquaintance, like going to a casual lunch or playing a simple board game, to gauge how well they get along.

This measured pace allows Taurus to avoid friendships that are not right for them. While it can take longer, it often results in deeper, more stable bonds.

The Core Traits Taurus Brings to Friendships

A Taurus friend can be recognized by certain key traits:

Loyalty: Once a Taurus considers you a friend, they are likely to stay by your side through many ups and downs. They typically show their loyalty through consistent actions, such as being available to help, or simply offering a listening ear.

Reliability: Taurus is known for keeping promises. If they say they will be there to support you for an important event or help you with a project, you can trust they will show up.

Patience and Calmness: In many cases, Taurus handles small conflicts and everyday challenges with composure. They rarely rush to end a friendship because of minor problems. Instead, they give friends time to work through issues.

Appreciation for Shared Comfort: Taurus often enjoys cozy and relaxed settings. Whether it is watching a show together on a couch, sharing a hearty meal, or strolling through a park, they enjoy activities that let them feel at ease.

These traits can make a Taurus a supportive, dependable friend who is ready to stand with you when you need them.

Communication Style with Friends

In conversations, a Taurus may speak in a steady, even tone. They are often good listeners who pay attention to details. They might not talk for hours about their private thoughts unless they trust the other person deeply. However, when they feel secure, they can open up and share stories, opinions, or personal reflections.

Honest but Careful: Taurus does not usually sugarcoat important truths, but they also do not like to hurt others. They might speak honestly while still trying to avoid conflict.

Preference for Direct Contact: Some Taurus individuals prefer face-to-face talks or phone calls over endless texting. This does not mean they dislike texting, but a steady, real conversation can feel more meaningful to them.

Unrushed Replies: If you ask a Taurus for their opinion, you might need to wait a moment. They often think before they speak, making sure they give a thoughtful response.

4. Taurus and Group Dynamics

When Taurus is part of a bigger friend group, they often play the role of the steady anchor. They might not lead every outing or plan all the details, but they offer a calm presence that helps keep everyone grounded. If the group is making decisions, a Taurus might lean toward the option that is most practical or that gives everyone a sense of comfort.

Peacemaker: In the group, Taurus might step in quietly if tensions rise, offering a calm viewpoint and trying to bring people back to a friendlier mood.

Steady Planner: While they might not be the most adventurous planners, they are good at ensuring that everyone stays informed about times, locations, or budgets.

Supportive Member: They might help set up events or bring supplies, doing their part without craving special attention.

However, if someone tries to push an idea that Taurus strongly dislikes, the group might notice their quiet but firm resistance. They typically prefer group plans that fit well into their sense of stability.

How Taurus Handles Friendship Conflicts

No friendship is perfect. When disagreements happen, Taurus might react in different ways depending on the situation:

Initial Calm: Often, Taurus will stay patient and try to listen to the other person's viewpoint. They do not enjoy loud fights, so they might quietly attempt to clarify the problem.

Steadfast Opinions: If they feel strongly about something, they can be quite firm. This can cause friction if their friend wants them to change their mind quickly.

Slow Resolution: Taurus might need time to accept that they made a mistake or to fully forgive a friend who has hurt them. They do not usually handle emotional changes overnight.

If the conflict grows big or involves a deep betrayal, Taurus may be hesitant to move past it. It is important for their friend to offer genuine apologies, clear explanations, and patience, letting Taurus process the issue at their own pace.

Activities Taurus Often Enjoys with Friends

Because Taurus is linked with the senses and comfort, they tend to enjoy simple, cozy pastimes when hanging out with friends. Some might include:

Dining: Good meals are often a favorite, whether cooking at home or going to a nice, laid-back restaurant. Taurus might take joy in picking out tasty dishes or sampling different flavors.

Calm Outdoors: A gentle walk in a park, visiting a scenic spot, or having a small picnic can appeal to Taurus's earthy side. They can recharge in a setting that is both peaceful and natural.

Arts and Crafts: Many Taurus people like hands-on tasks, such as painting, pottery, knitting, or other creative hobbies. Sharing this time with friends can be a pleasant bonding experience.

Movie Nights or Board Games: Staying in with popcorn or playing an old board game can make a Taurus feel at ease and connected with friends.

Music and Concerts: Some Taurus folks appreciate good music and may attend concerts or local shows with friends, as long as the environment is not too chaotic.

These activities fit well with Taurus's preference for comfort and practicality. They are generally not drawn to wild or high-risk adventures with friends unless they have strong placements in other zodiac signs that add more spontaneity.

Building Trust Over Time

Taurus does not trust easily. They often need to see consistent behavior from a friend before they feel safe enough to share deeper thoughts or personal worries. This slow trust-building process might look like:

Observing Consistency: Taurus watches to see if a friend keeps their word, respects boundaries, and remains the same person across different situations.

Small Steps of Sharing: They might reveal a little bit about themselves, then wait to see how the friend reacts. If the friend is supportive, they might open up more next time.

Acts of Support: Taurus may test trust by offering help or seeing if the friend is there to help them in return during small challenges.

Once trust is established, Taurus can be a loyal companion who is willing to stand by a friend even when things get rough. But if the trust is broken, it can be difficult for Taurus to feel the same closeness again.

Friendship Compatibility with Other Signs

Although any sign can be friends with any other sign, people often wonder which signs might get along best with Taurus. Here are some general thoughts:

Other Earth Signs (Virgo, Capricorn): They share Taurus's practicality, making it easier to agree on daily plans. They often find comfort in structured, calm activities.

Water Signs (Cancer, Scorpio, Pisces): Water signs can offer emotional depth, while Taurus offers stability. Cancer and Pisces might soothe Taurus's worries, and Scorpio shares a certain strong-willed vibe, though that can lead to power clashes if not handled gently.

Air Signs (Gemini, Libra, Aquarius): Air signs bring fresh ideas and social energy, which can be fun for Taurus as long as the quick pace does not overwhelm them. Libra, also ruled by Venus, might share an interest in harmony.

Fire Signs (Aries, Leo, Sagittarius): Fire signs can encourage Taurus to try livelier activities, and Taurus can help them slow down when needed. However, if a fire sign wants to change plans too often, Taurus could feel uneasy.

Again, these are only broad ideas. True friendship depends on the individuals, shared interests, and willingness to respect each other's differences.

Dealing with Friendship Challenges

Even strong bonds can face tests. Here are some challenges Taurus might meet in friendships and how they might approach them:

Different Social Needs: If a friend wants to go out every night, but Taurus prefers to stay in and rest, they might need to compromise on a plan that suits both or meet less often but share quality time.

Conflict Over Pace: Taurus moves slowly, while some friends move fast. This can create frustration. Talking openly about comfort levels and scheduling can help.

Emotional Distance: Because Taurus takes time to show their inner feelings, some friends might see them as uninterested or cold. Open communication can clear up misunderstandings.

Financial Disagreements: Taurus values stability and might be more cautious with spending. If a friend is more carefree, they might disagree on how to split costs or choose activities that fit both budgets.

In all these cases, honest conversation and a willingness to see the friend's point of view can smooth out the issues. Taurus is often ready to give and receive kindness if they feel respected.

Maintaining Long-Term Friendships

Many Taurus people keep friends for a long time once a bond is formed. They enjoy the comfort of familiar faces and shared memories. Here are some ways Taurus typically supports these connections:

Steady Contact: Even if they do not see their friend every day, Taurus might call, send messages, or plan a meet-up regularly. They like the idea of a predictable rhythm in friendships.

Acts of Service: Taurus may show friendship through helpful actions—offering a ride, preparing a meal, or helping to fix something.

Respect for Boundaries: They generally do not push friends to share more than they want. They can handle a slow reveal of personal stories or secrets, and they expect the same respect for their own boundaries.

Shared Familiar Rituals: They might enjoy repeating a favorite activity, such as meeting at the same spot each month or enjoying a cozy movie night. This sense of continuity can keep the bond strong over time.

Signs That a Taurus Trusts You

If you are wondering whether you have reached a deeper level of friendship with a Taurus, here are some signs to look for:

Sharing Personal Feelings: They start talking about deeper worries, joys, or family matters, trusting you to handle that information carefully.

Relaxed Body Language: You might see them looking more at ease, leaning in closer during talks, or even joking around in a calm, genuine way.

Willingness to Try Something New with You: If a Taurus is normally cautious but decides to join you for an unfamiliar activity, it shows they trust you to keep them safe or comfortable.

Inviting You into Their "Home Base": This could mean inviting you to their actual home, a special hangout spot, or introducing you to their closest circle of friends.

When a Friendship Breaks Down

Sadly, not all friendships last. A Taurus might end a friendship or let it fade if:

Trust Is Broken: If a friend betrays their confidence, lies, or hurts them deeply, Taurus can find it hard to forgive.

Repetitive Conflict: Constant arguments can wear out a Taurus who wants stability.

Lack of Mutual Effort: If Taurus feels they are always the one reaching out, they might step back and see if the other person returns the interest. If not, they will likely move on.

When a Taurus chooses to step away, they usually do it quietly. They might not want to engage in a dramatic confrontation. Instead, they might gradually reduce contact. It is important to note that if a friend sincerely tries to repair the bond, Taurus might be open to giving things another shot—provided they see genuine change and enough time to mend the hurt.

Helping a Taurus Friend During Tough Times

If you have a Taurus friend going through a rough patch, you can support them in ways that suit their nature:

Offer Steady Presence: Instead of grand gestures, let them know you are there if they want to talk or need a bit of help.

Practical Support: Ask if they need errands done, or if you can take on a small task that is stressing them out. Sometimes simple, concrete help is more meaningful to Taurus than lengthy pep talks.

Respect Their Privacy: If they do not want to share all the details, do not push them. Show that you are available without prying.

Suggest Comforting Outings: Think of calm activities—like going for a gentle walk, visiting a quiet cafe, or watching a relaxing movie at home.

When a Taurus feels consistently supported and not rushed, they are more likely to trust you and see you as someone they can depend on

Signs a Taurus Might Be Upset in a Friendship

Taurus is not always vocal about their frustrations. They may try to maintain peace until they hit a limit. A few warning signs:

Withdrawal: They start avoiding meet-ups or respond to messages much slower.

Short, Terse Replies: If a Taurus who usually communicates in a friendly way becomes curt, it can hint at hidden stress or annoyance.

Body Language: They might close themselves off physically, avoid eye contact, or show tension when you are around.

Quiet Resentment: Sometimes they hold onto negative feelings, and it can show up in subtle ways, like not laughing at a shared joke or not engaging in normal conversation.

If you suspect a Taurus friend is unhappy, it can help to approach them gently, ask if everything is okay, and let them know you want to understand their viewpoint.

Helping Taurus Open Up Socially

Some Taurus individuals are more private and might benefit from a nudge to explore new social opportunities:

Suggest Low-Stress Gatherings: Invite them to events with a small group, rather than large, noisy parties.

Encourage Shared Interests: If you find a club or local group that centers on art, nature, or a relaxed hobby, they might be more open to joining.

Show Them the Benefits: Talk about how meeting others can lead to pleasant friendships or interesting exchanges, focusing on how it can be stable and comfortable, rather than full of unknowns.

Taurus will usually join if they see that the environment matches their comfort level or interests. Once there, they may form strong connections over time.

Taurus Friends and Long-Distance Connections

Friendships do not always stay in the same town or city. Taurus is often capable of keeping long-distance bonds steady if they believe the connection is worthwhile:

- **Predictable Schedules**: They might prefer to have a set day or time for a phone call, video chat, or message exchange.

- **Thoughtful Packages**: Sending small tokens like snacks, letters, or handmade items can help maintain a sense of closeness despite distance.

- **Honest Updates**: Taurus appreciates sincerity. Sharing real-life news, rather than vague or filtered versions, helps keep trust alive.

They may not be the type to message constantly, but they will usually keep the connection alive if the bond feels genuine.

Taurus as a Supportive Friend

When a friend faces difficulties, Taurus can offer a type of steady and patient help:

Listening Ear: They are often willing to sit quietly and let you talk about your worries.

Calm Solutions: If asked for advice, they might offer practical suggestions that can be tried in real life.

Physical Comfort: Some Taurus folks might offer a hug or a reassuring hand on the shoulder if that is acceptable, showing warmth through gentle touch.

Long-Term Encouragement: They do not expect immediate changes. They can encourage friends to handle challenges slowly and with care.

This approach can feel comforting to many, though friends who want fast changes might sometimes see Taurus's patient style as too slow.

The Downside: Stubbornness in Friendship

We discussed stubbornness as a general trait in earlier chapters, but it can specifically affect friendships. For instance, if Taurus feels their friend acted unfairly, they might hold onto that feeling and refuse to see the friend's side. Also, if a friend suggests a new hobby or a different activity, Taurus might resist trying it just because they dislike change.

Friends who want to keep things flexible might find it challenging to bend a Taurus friend's firm perspective. Still, if they approach Taurus with understanding, show real interest in their comfort, and provide logical reasons for trying something new, Taurus can open up. Patience on both sides is key.

Balancing Alone Time and Friendship Time

Taurus often needs a balance between social interactions and personal quiet time. This sign's calm nature can get drained if they are around people too often, especially if the environment is noisy. As a friend of a Taurus, it is wise to:

Respect Their Need for Space: Do not take it personally if they say they would rather stay in one evening.

Plan Ahead: Taurus generally likes to know about gatherings or events with some notice, so they can set their schedule and preserve their sense of order.

Understand Slow Social Rhythms: They might not be the friend who is constantly available. But when they do spend time with you, they give it genuine attention.

Final Thoughts on Taurus in Friendships

Taurus brings honesty, calm, and steadiness to friendships. They are likely to be the friend who remembers details about your life, stays through hard times, and looks for ways to share small comforts. While their caution in forming new bonds and their resistance to sudden changes can slow down the start of a friendship, once a Taurus truly connects with someone, they often prove to be a faithful companion.

By understanding these traits, friends of Taurus can create an environment that supports stable connections and mutual respect. Likewise, Taurus individuals can stay aware of their tendency to become stubborn or overly private, practicing openness and flexibility when it is truly needed. With a balanced approach, Taurus can form lifelong friendships that bring comfort, trust, and shared happiness to all involved.

CHAPTER 8: TAURUS IN FAMILY LIFE

Family is often a major source of belonging and security for many people, including Taurus. Known for loyalty, practicality, and a steady demeanor, Taurus tends to play specific roles within the family unit. These roles can differ based on whether Taurus is a child, sibling, parent, or extended relative, but the desire for stability is a common thread. In this chapter, we will look at how Taurus typically behaves within different family positions, how they manage conflicts at home, and how they prefer to maintain a calm, comforting household.

The Importance of Family for Taurus

Taurus often sees home and family as a firm foundation. This sign values the sense of being rooted in a familiar place with people they trust. They feel more at peace in environments where they know what to expect day after day. Because of this, many Taurus individuals put effort into creating a comfortable, welcoming space for their loved ones. They may:

Treasure Shared Routines: Having meals at a regular time, spending evenings in the living room, or going to local events with family can be soothing to Taurus.

Care About Security: Taurus might be keen to ensure the family has enough money saved for emergencies or that the home feels safe and well-kept.

Enjoy Familiar Home Activities: Whether it is a quiet evening reading or a family-style dinner, Taurus finds warmth in repeated home-based habits.

This deep connection to stability often leads Taurus to become a grounding presence in their family.

Taurus as a Child

A Taurus child may show signs of their steady nature from a young age. They might enjoy simple joys, like playing with blocks, drawing pictures, or engaging in calm, hands-on tasks. Some ways a Taurus child might stand out:

Routine Lovers: They feel safe when the daily schedule is predictable. If bedtime or mealtime changes abruptly, they might get upset until they adapt.

Material Attachments: They might have a favorite blanket or toy that they hold onto for a long time, seeing it as a source of comfort.

Soft-Hearted Yet Stubborn: They can be sweet and affectionate but can also dig in their heels if they do not want to do something. Patience from caregivers can help.

Parents of a Taurus child can encourage them by providing a stable environment. Gently showing them that small changes can be okay can help the child learn that not every change is bad. Praising them (in a calm, supportive way) for being patient or putting in steady effort can also help them feel appreciated.

Taurus as a Sibling

As a sibling, Taurus might take on the role of the calm presence in the household, or sometimes the quiet but firm one who does not like to be pushed. This can lead to different sibling dynamics:

- **Protective**: If a Taurus feels a younger sibling is being treated poorly, they may step in. Their reliable nature can make them a strong supporter if a sibling needs help.

- **Possessive**: They can be territorial about shared spaces, objects, or even parents' attention. If they feel a sibling is invading their safe zone, they might react strongly.

- **Conflict Handling**: They might avoid drama with siblings, unless someone keeps teasing them in a way that crosses their lines. Then, their stubborn side may appear, leading to arguments that last longer.

Open communication can help. For example, if siblings negotiate who uses certain items or how they share a room, Taurus can feel more at ease. Over time, they usually show devotion to their siblings, standing by them through life's ups and downs.

Taurus as a Parent

A Taurus parent often provides a calm, structured home. They want their children to feel safe, well-fed, and comfortable. Some traits of a Taurus parent include:

Consistency in Routines: They might keep regular mealtimes, bedtimes, and family rituals. This can help children feel secure.

Practical Support: A Taurus parent might teach children life skills, like cooking, budgeting, or gardening (if they have a yard), in a simple and hands-on way.

Firm Boundaries: While they can be gentle, Taurus parents can also be stubborn if children challenge important rules. They believe in setting clear guidelines for behavior.

Encouragement of Simple Pleasures: They might create family nights with homemade meals, board games, or calm outdoor activities, helping children enjoy a slower pace.

A potential downside is that a Taurus parent might resist a child's need for spontaneous exploration if it clashes with the parent's sense of order. Balancing the parent's love of stability with the child's curiosity can lead to healthy growth for everyone involved.

Taurus with Older Family Members

When dealing with grandparents or older relatives, Taurus usually shows respect and care. They can sit quietly and listen to stories from the past, and they might be willing to run errands or help with household tasks for older relatives who need support. Their calm and patient nature often allows them to connect with elders in a gentle way. However, if older relatives push for quick decisions or sudden changes, Taurus might become uneasy.

The Taurus Home Environment

Taurus places great importance on making the home environment relaxing and welcoming. They might:

Choose Soft Decorations: Cushions, soft rugs, warm lighting, or items that please the senses.

Focus on Tasty Meals: Good-quality ingredients and comforting dishes can be a highlight of a Taurus-run kitchen.

Prioritize Stability: They might plan finances carefully so the family can afford the comforts they love.

Enjoy Nature Elements: If possible, they might keep potted plants, a small herb patch, or fresh flowers to bring an earthy touch indoors.

A Taurus family member might be the one reminding everyone to remove their shoes at the door or to wash dishes right after eating, preserving the comfort and cleanliness that helps them feel at ease.

Handling Family Conflicts

No family is free from disagreements. Taurus often responds to family disputes with calmness at first, but if the argument continues or if they feel attacked, their stubbornness can emerge. They may:

Stay Quiet Initially: Observing the conflict, hoping it will pass.

Stand Firm on Core Values: If the argument challenges something they deeply believe in, they are unlikely to back down.

Need Time: Taurus may need a while to cool off and think after a fight. Pressing them for instant forgiveness or resolution can make them dig in further.

Seek a Peaceful Tone: If they notice family members raising their voices, they might suggest calmer communication, though they can also get frustrated if they feel unheard.

A healthy way to handle conflict with a Taurus in the family is to speak honestly but gently, allowing them to process information and express their viewpoint without feeling rushed.

Taurus and Family Traditions

Because Taurus values continuity, they might enjoy any form of repeated family event or shared practice. They could take pleasure in consistent gatherings at certain times of the year, though they might not call it a special word. Even a weekly meal can become special if it happens regularly with loved ones. Taurus might be the one reminding everyone to keep these events or tasks on the calendar, since they see them as an anchor of togetherness.

Financial Habits Within the Family

Taurus is known for being careful with money. In a family context, they might:

Budget for Basics First: Ensuring the house bills, groceries, and other essentials are covered.

Save for Comfort Items: They might put aside money over time to buy a better mattress, a nicer sofa, or improvements around the home that add warmth.

Avoid Rash Spending: They might prefer to research major purchases carefully, which can annoy family members who want quick decisions.

Teach Money Skills: If they are parents or older siblings, they might guide younger relatives on how to handle an allowance or a first job paycheck sensibly.

On the other hand, if they go too far with their love of comforts, some Taurus individuals could be tempted to buy more than they really need. Striking a balance between saving and occasional treats is key.

Taurus and Extended Family Gatherings

When the wider family comes together—cousins, aunts, uncles—Taurus might:

Focus on Practical Preparations: They often volunteer to help set up, bring dishes, or make sure chairs and tables are arranged.

Seek Familiar Faces: They might gravitate to the relatives they know best. While they can be polite to everyone, they feel more at ease with those who share their calm approach.

Need Quiet Time: Large family events can be loud. Taurus may step outside for some air or find a quieter corner to avoid feeling overwhelmed.

They usually appreciate the sense of belonging that extended family offers, but they can feel tired if the event lasts too long or involves lots of changes in plans. Maintaining a stable environment, even in a bigger gathering, helps Taurus enjoy the occasion.

Supporting a Taurus Family Member

If you have a Taurus in your family and want to offer them help or kindness, consider these tips:

Respect Their Routine: Try not to force them to rearrange schedules on short notice. If a change is needed, explain it clearly and give them time to adjust.

Offer Calm Talk: If you need to discuss a serious matter, pick a moment when the Taurus family member is relaxed and open to a steady conversation.

Give Practical Assistance: A Taurus might appreciate help with physical tasks, such as organizing a space, cooking, or running errands, especially during stressful times.

Show Genuine Appreciation: When they make a comforting meal or tidy a common area, a sincere "thank you" can reassure them that their efforts are valued.

Taurus Coping with Family Stress

Life events like moving, financial problems, or health issues can stress a Taurus. They might respond by:

Holding onto What Is Familiar: They cling more to routines, daily rituals, or personal items that give them a feeling of safety.

Growing More Quiet: They may speak less about their worries, appearing calm on the surface but anxious underneath.

Seeking Practical Solutions: Taurus might look for a stable plan to solve the problem step by step, though they can get stuck if the situation is too chaotic.

Needing Gentle Emotional Support: They might not openly ask for hugs or reassurances, but they appreciate family members who sense when they need a calm presence or a kind word.

Encouraging them to share worries in a private conversation can help, as it allows them to voice concerns without feeling exposed in a big group.

The Taurus Teenager Phase

Teenage years can be a period of strong emotions. For a Taurus teen, you might notice:

Desire for Autonomy: They want their space and might resist if parents or siblings try to control every detail of their lives.

Stubborn Rebellions: If they feel forced into something they dislike, they can dig in their heels for a long time.

Focus on Personal Comfort: A Taurus teen might spend time making their room a cozy retreat—decorating with favorite pillows, choosing soft lighting, and playing music they find soothing.

Slow Emotional Sharing: They may not quickly tell parents or siblings about crushes, friendship issues, or personal dreams, needing to be sure they will not be judged.

Allowing them some independence while guiding them with patience can keep conflicts from intensifying. Clear, consistent rules paired with calm discussions often work better than harsh or sudden punishments.

Balancing Different Family Personalities

In a family, every member might have a unique zodiac sign and traits. Taurus can blend well with relatives who appreciate calm stability. However, they might clash with family members who always want excitement or who change plans on a whim. Strategies for balance can include:

- **Open Discussion of Preferences**: If a sibling or parent is very spontaneous, they can plan at least part of the weekend to match Taurus's comfort level, while leaving some room for surprises.

- **Shared Activities**: Finding a middle ground, like a calm outing that still includes a little newness, can keep both sides happy.

- **Respecting Boundaries**: If a relative is loud or pushes Taurus to do things quickly, Taurus might kindly ask for a slower pace or some notice beforehand.

When the family understands that Taurus thrives on steadiness, they can adapt their plans in small ways to make everyone feel included.

Taurus and Family Health Matters

Because Taurus rules the neck and throat area (in traditional astrology), there is sometimes a focus on physical wellness. More generally, a Taurus in the family might:

- **Enjoy Tasty, Comforting Foods**: But might need to watch out for overindulging.

- **Prefer Mild Exercise**: They might like walking, stretching, or yoga over high-impact sports.

- **Look After Loved Ones' Health**: They might gently remind others to wear a coat in cold weather or to have a healthy meal.

If health issues appear in the family, Taurus is likely to tackle them by following a consistent routine, scheduling regular check-ups, and making small, steady lifestyle adjustments rather than huge shifts all at once.

Cultural or Religious Family Practices

If the family has certain cultural or religious customs, Taurus may be one of the main supporters of these. They might help keep the family's traditions alive, because they see these customs as a link to their roots. This can bring them a sense of continuity. Sometimes, however, if the family wants to modernize these customs too quickly, Taurus might feel uneasy. A gradual approach that respects the old ways can help them adjust.

Conflict Between Generations

When family members from different generations share a home, conflict can arise around technology use, house rules, or ways of thinking. A Taurus might find it frustrating if older relatives cling to traditions too strongly, or if younger relatives dismiss traditions too fast. That said, Taurus often acts as a bridge by offering:

- **Empathy**: They can listen to each side, understanding the desire for stability (from older relatives) and the wish for change (from younger ones).

- **Respectful Advice**: If asked, Taurus might propose a slow shift that keeps some elements of tradition while allowing new ideas.

- **Willingness to Set an Example**: They might show, through small steps, how to accept a bit of change without throwing out everything familiar.

Taurus in a Large or Small Family Setting

- **Large Family**: In big families, Taurus might focus on a close circle of relatives they feel most comfortable with. They may help by doing steady tasks—like cleaning up, planning meals, or helping younger members. However, the noise and chaos might sometimes make them retreat.

- **Small Family**: In a household with just a few members, Taurus can really shine. They have fewer competing opinions to handle, so they can build a calm, stable routine more easily.

Each setup has benefits and drawbacks, but Taurus generally values a sense of calm that can be easier to find in smaller settings or through well-organized routines.

Passing on Taurus Values to the Next Generation

Taurus values can be passed down in simple, everyday ways:

Steady Routines: Children or younger relatives learn that keeping to a regular meal or bedtime helps everyone feel stable.

Respect for the Senses: Teaching them to notice pleasant smells, tastes, or sights, so they learn to appreciate little comforts in life.

Practical Skills: Showing them how to handle money wisely, cook balanced meals, or maintain a neat living space.

Loyalty to Loved Ones: Modeling what it means to stand by each other during hard times, and to keep promises.

These lessons can help younger family members grow up with a grounded sense of security and a healthy respect for simple joys.

CHAPTER 9: TAURUS IN WORK LIFE

Work is a big part of life for many people. Whether someone works in an office, a store, on a farm, or at home, the way they do their job can show their strengths, weaknesses, and personal style. For Taurus, certain traits often stand out in the workplace. They are known for steadiness, practicality, and a strong sense of responsibility. In this chapter, we will look at how Taurus behaves as an employee, a leader, or a teammate, and we will explore how Taurus handles work tasks, deadlines, and stress. We will also see how Taurus might select or thrive in certain types of jobs and how they can address some of the common hurdles they face at work.

Why Taurus Approach to Work Is Unique

Taurus is usually linked with stability and a desire for security. At work, this can mean they want a position that feels consistent. They might not be too comfortable in roles that change every day or that bring many unexpected challenges. Instead, they often seek a job where they can learn a routine, do their tasks well, and build a long-term future. This outlook can be very helpful in fields where patience, careful attention, and reliability are important.

However, this same steadiness can also make it tough for Taurus to handle sudden changes. If a boss decides to switch the entire process or system at the last moment, Taurus might feel uneasy. They prefer planning ahead and focusing on proven methods. Still, once they have learned a new system and see how it works in real life, they can adapt and keep going.

Common Taurus Traits That Show Up at Work

Reliability
Taurus generally shows up on time, does what they promise, and follows through on tasks. Managers often appreciate having someone they can trust to complete assignments consistently.

Patience
If a project takes a long time or requires many steps, Taurus can stick with it without losing interest quickly. This patience can make them good at detail-oriented tasks.

Practical Thinking
Taurus often likes solutions that are tried and tested. They look for methods that work in the real world. This can be a benefit in jobs where safety, efficiency, or consistency matter.

Steadiness Under Stress
While Taurus can feel pressure, they usually try to handle it in a calm way. They might take deep breaths, focus on one task at a time, and avoid panic.

Stubbornness
At times, the Taurus refusal to change or compromise can create difficulties. They might dig in their heels if asked to switch a process they believe is fine as it is.

Taurus as an Employee

As an employee, Taurus tends to do well in environments where roles are clearly defined. They want to know what is expected of them, the steps to follow, and any deadlines they need to meet. Once they have this information, they can follow the routine carefully and often produce consistent results.

Focus on the Task: Taurus employees usually prefer to finish one job before moving on to the next. If the workplace has too many sudden interruptions, they may become uneasy.

Respect for Structure: They often respect a chain of command. If they trust their manager, they will try hard to meet that manager's standards.

Loyalty to the Company: If they feel valued, a Taurus employee might stay in the same position or company for many years. They like the comfort of knowing their workplace, and they enjoy building expertise over time.

Caution with Risk: Taurus employees may not jump into risky moves unless they see clear, solid reasons. They prefer to avoid mistakes that come from rushing.

Taurus employees can be an asset because they bring a sense of consistency. On the other hand, if the environment changes too often, or if they feel they cannot trust their boss, they might become withdrawn or stubborn.

Taurus as a Manager or Leader

When a Taurus takes a leadership role, they often apply similar qualities to guide their team:

Steady Expectations: They tend to set clear rules and routines. Their team usually knows what they need to do because Taurus leaders like structure.

Focus on Practical Methods: Rather than chasing every new idea, a Taurus manager often picks approaches with a record of success. They want to see evidence that something will work before they invest resources.

Patience with Team Members: If a team member needs extra time to learn a skill, a Taurus leader may offer steady support, provided they see real effort.

Possible Drawback—Resistance to Innovation: Sometimes, a Taurus manager may be slow to adopt new technology or methods, especially if they are comfortable with the current way of working.

In general, Taurus leaders prefer a calm, orderly setting. They can help workers feel at ease because people know what is expected. But they might need to be mindful of situations that require quick decisions or big shifts, making sure they do not hold back progress.

Preferred Work Environments

Taurus typically likes workplaces where they have a certain amount of predictability. It does not have to be an old-fashioned job; it could be a modern office, a restaurant, or a creative studio. The key is that day-to-day tasks are at least somewhat regular. Here are a few preferences:

Stable Roles: Knowing their role and duties clearly makes Taurus feel more comfortable. Vague or rapidly shifting roles can cause stress.

Comfortable Setup: Taurus tends to appreciate a desk that is not too cramped, a chair that feels good, or tools that are well-organized. Small comforts can keep them motivated.

Realistic Goals: If deadlines or goals are set at a steady pace, Taurus feels confident. Unrealistic or constantly changing deadlines may wear them out.

Fair Compensation: Financial security is often important to Taurus. If they feel underpaid or uncertain about pay, they might lose trust in the organization.

Workplaces that respect these preferences can bring out the best in Taurus. Of course, not all jobs offer perfect stability. In that case, Taurus may adapt if they see the value in doing so. However, they will need time to adjust to major changes.

Handling Deadlines and Pressure

Taurus is often patient, but deadlines can create stress if the tasks are not planned well. Since they prefer a steady approach, they do best with:

Clear Schedules: If a manager sets a clear timeline, Taurus can plan their steps. They typically do not like last-minute rushing.

Step-by-Step Tasks: Breaking a project into smaller parts fits well with Taurus's steady style. They can complete each stage carefully before moving on.

Avoiding Procrastination: Because they move at a measured pace, waiting until the last minute can lead to stress. It helps if Taurus starts tasks early enough to finish comfortably.

Calm Problem-Solving: If an unexpected problem appears, Taurus usually tackles it methodically, as long as they have the tools or information needed.

When a situation demands immediate responses or big changes in direction, Taurus may feel unsettled. Still, once they realize that quick action is required, many can step up as long as the change is explained well. They might need a bit of extra reassurance or instructions to feel sure of the new path.

Communication Style at Work

In the workplace, Taurus usually communicates in a direct but polite manner. They might not always volunteer their opinions unless asked, but when they do speak, they prefer clarity.

Listening Skills: Taurus often pays attention when others speak, especially if the topic involves practical matters. They might not interrupt unless it is really important.

Saying "No" Politely: If asked to do something they see as unrealistic, they may push back calmly, explaining their reasons. This can come off as stubborn at times.

Written vs. Verbal: Some Taurus individuals appreciate emails or written notes because they can think about the information before responding. They may also keep these messages for reference.

Diplomacy: While not always flashy with words, Taurus can be tactful. They do not usually enjoy big arguments, so they try to remain polite, unless they feel cornered.

When working in teams, Taurus often waits to see if everyone else is on the same page. If they sense confusion, they might offer a straightforward plan for the group. They might say something like, "How about we list the steps we need, then assign each step to a person?" This helps ground the discussion in practical action.

Teamwork and Collaboration

Taurus can be a strong teammate because of their reliability and willingness to do their share. They often want to make sure the group is organized, and they are comfortable focusing on a specific piece of the project. However, challenges can come up when:

Other Team Members Move Too Fast: If colleagues switch direction repeatedly, a Taurus might get frustrated.

Creative Brainstorms with No Plan: Taurus might feel unsettled in a discussion that only involves wild ideas and no plan for making them happen.

Pressure to Compromise Too Quickly: If asked to change their part of the project without a good explanation, a Taurus might resist.

Still, if the team clarifies goals and roles, Taurus usually cooperates well. They can be the one who keeps the project on track. Others might bring big ideas, while Taurus helps shape those ideas into real tasks.

Suitable Careers for Taurus

There is no single job that every Taurus will love, but certain fields might appeal because of the sign's traits. Some Taurus individuals do well in:

Accounting or Finance: This can appeal to Taurus's desire for stability and careful handling of money.

Real Estate or Property Management: They might like helping people find homes or maintain properties, where steadiness and physical comfort matter.

Culinary Arts: Many Taurus folks enjoy good food and the process of cooking. Working as a chef or baker can give them a place to share that passion.

Gardening, Agriculture, or Landscaping: Being an earth sign, Taurus might enjoy hands-on work with plants, soil, and nature, though not every Taurus chooses this path.

Design or Crafts: Creating beautiful but practical items can blend their sense of aesthetics and practicality.

Administration or Office Management: They can maintain order, schedules, and procedures.

Engineering or Architecture: This depends on other skills, but Taurus's patient, thorough nature can suit fields that require precision.

These are just examples. Taurus can thrive in many roles if they feel there is a stable process and a sense of security or a clear plan for growth.

Dealing with Work Conflicts

Even in the best workplaces, conflicts can happen. Taurus typically tries to avoid constant arguments, but if a dispute arises, they might:

Stay Calm at First: They often maintain a quiet demeanor while they listen to the other side.

Stick Firmly to Their Position: If they believe they are correct, they can seem unmovable. Sometimes, they need strong proof or a clear explanation to change their mind.

Seek a Practical Solution: Taurus might suggest a compromise that involves concrete steps. However, if the other person seems purely emotional or unorganized, Taurus may have trouble finding common ground.

Need Some Time: If they feel attacked or insulted, they might hold onto hurt feelings. A calm and respectful apology or discussion later can help them let go of grudges.

For managers or coworkers who want to resolve a conflict with Taurus, it helps to approach them with facts and suggestions for a stable solution. Yelling or abrupt changes are likely to cause Taurus to pull back or resist.

Leadership Style in Groups or Projects

When Taurus takes on a leadership position, they often:

Set Clear Schedules: They prefer to map out deadlines and tasks in a way that is easy to follow.

Make Practical Assignments: Instead of giving vague responsibilities, they try to match tasks with people's strengths.

Stay Available: They might not hover, but they are ready to answer questions or step in with guidance.

Expect Reliability from Others: Because they hold themselves to a certain level of reliability, they also expect that from team members.

This style can work well in organizations that value routine or consistent output. However, if the project demands quick, creative pivots, Taurus might feel out of their element as a leader unless they have a second-in-command who thrives on rapid changes.

Balancing Personal Life with Work

Taurus usually values a good balance between work and personal time. They believe that having a stable home life helps them be more effective at work. Because they value comfort and relaxation, they might not enjoy jobs that demand extremely long hours with no rest.

Seeking Steady Schedules: Taurus often prefers jobs with set hours rather than ones that change every day.

Protecting Rest Time: They might choose to leave work on time to recharge at home, enjoying quiet hobbies or time with loved ones.

Avoiding Overwork: If a job pushes them to extreme stress, a Taurus might eventually look for a calmer position. They recognize that money and security are important, but they also want a life that feels balanced.

In modern times, many workplaces encourage flexible hours or remote work, which can help Taurus manage their pace. However, Taurus might also do well with a traditional office schedule if it allows them to keep clear boundaries between work and rest.

Growing a Taurus's Career Over Time

Because Taurus appreciates slow, steady progress, they might seek a career path that lets them climb step by step. They can build strong expertise if they stay in one field or company for a long time. Over time, they might rise into positions that reward their loyalty and knowledge. Some ways Taurus can grow:

Gaining Certificates or Further Training: They often do well when learning structured skills that improve their job performance.

Seeking Mentors: A practical mentor who can show them real-world methods might be very helpful.

Expanding Their Network: Taurus might not be a big social butterfly, but forming relationships with coworkers and industry contacts can create a solid support system for future opportunities.

Embracing Some Change: If they stay stuck in the same role for too long, they might miss better chances. Learning to accept certain shifts can lead to advancement.

Potential Pitfalls for Taurus at Work

While Taurus has many strengths, a few pitfalls can hinder them if not managed:

Overly Resistant to Change: If a workplace updates systems often, Taurus might struggle. They could become labeled as resistant or slow.

Holding onto Grudges: Personal conflicts that are not resolved can affect teamwork if Taurus will not let go of past issues.

Fear of Taking Risks: Taurus might pass up a promotion or new challenge if it feels too uncertain. This caution keeps them safe but can limit growth.

Rigid Mindset: When they decide on a method, they may ignore suggestions that could improve efficiency.

By being aware of these tendencies, Taurus can try to soften them when needed, staying open to proven new ideas and letting go of resentments more quickly.

Tips for Taurus to Succeed at Work

Embrace Small Adjustments: Practice making little changes to your routine from time to time. It can help you adapt when bigger changes happen.

Seek Clear Communication: If you feel unsure about a task, ask questions early. This prevents confusion and helps you avoid doing extra work later.

Stay Organized: Use planners or digital tools to map out your tasks and deadlines, matching your steady approach.

Find a Mentor: Look for someone whose calm, practical style you respect. Their advice might fit well with your own.

Balance Comfort with Growth: It is good to find roles that feel stable, but remember to watch for chances to learn and move forward.

Address Issues Early: If you sense tension with a coworker or manager, speak up in a calm manner before resentment builds.

Working with a Taurus

If you have a Taurus colleague or direct report, here are some ideas to keep things running smoothly:

Provide a Predictable Structure: Share deadlines and processes in advance. Avoid constant last-minute requests if you can.

Offer Logical Explanations: When changes happen, explain why. Taurus is more likely to adapt if the reasoning makes sense.

Respect Their Pace: They work best when they can move at a steady speed without feeling rushed.

Encourage Input: They may have practical ideas, so invite them to share thoughts. They might not speak up unless asked.

Resolve Conflicts Calmly: If arguments come up, approach them politely, using facts rather than yelling.

Acknowledge Achievements: Taurus appreciates recognition for steady results. A simple statement like "We appreciate your consistency" can mean a lot.

Handling Burnout or Stress

Even though Taurus is usually patient, they can experience burnout if their workload becomes overwhelming. Signs might include fatigue, loss of interest, or irritability. To avoid or recover from burnout:

Take Scheduled Breaks: A few minutes to stretch or relax can help Taurus feel grounded.

Maintain Sleep Routines: Adequate rest is vital for their calm nature.

Speak with Supervisors: If tasks are too heavy or deadlines too tight, a calm conversation might lead to adjustments.

Try Soothing Activities: Simple exercises, walks in nature, or a nice snack can bring back a sense of comfort during a hectic day.

Taurus and Entrepreneurship

Some Taurus individuals might start their own business if they have a solid plan. Because they are good at managing resources and sticking to a schedule, they can run a stable business over time. Possible pitfalls include:

Taking Too Long to Launch: They might research and plan endlessly, nervous about risks.

Difficulty with Quick Market Changes: If a market shifts rapidly, Taurus might struggle to pivot swiftly.

Strong Work Ethic: On the positive side, their patience can pay off, especially if the business requires careful building of a client base.

If Taurus entrepreneurs balance their caution with the willingness to adapt, they can succeed in fields that match their practical mindset.

Mixing Personal and Professional Boundaries

Taurus values security in all areas of life. Mixing personal friendships and work can be tricky. Some Taurus individuals are careful about sharing private information with coworkers. They may keep clear lines, so that if work conflicts arise, personal bonds are not harmed. Others might form close ties at work over time, especially if they trust people. Either way, Taurus likes to keep a sense of control and comfort. If work becomes too personal or dramatic, they may pull back to maintain stability.

CHAPTER 10: TAURUS AND MONEY

Money is often connected with security and comfort, two things that Taurus deeply values. Having enough savings, a reliable income, and sensible spending habits can help Taurus feel calm and at ease. On the other hand, money problems can create stress for any person, but especially for Taurus, who likes to know they are financially protected. In this chapter, we will look at how Taurus usually handles money, from saving and budgeting to big purchases and risk-taking. We will also discuss common financial pitfalls and ways Taurus can balance their need for comfort with wise, long-term financial plans.

Why Money Matters to Taurus

For many Taurus individuals, money is not just about numbers—it is about feeling safe. Knowing that bills are paid and there is a cushion for emergencies can help them relax and enjoy life's comforts. It does not mean all Taurus folks are wealthy or driven only by money. Rather, they see money as a tool that supports the stability they cherish. Without a secure financial base, Taurus might feel uneasy or worried.

This attitude can show up in different ways. Some Taurus individuals will work hard to build savings, while others might try to earn extra income through side jobs or investments. However they approach it, the main aim is often the same: to ensure they can meet daily needs without constant financial stress, and possibly afford occasional treats or items that bring them joy.

The Taurus View on Budgeting

Taurus is often practical and patient, which can make them fairly good at budgeting if they choose to focus on it. They usually approach budgeting by:

Listing Basic Expenses: Such as housing, food, utilities, and transportation. Taurus wants to see exactly how much is needed for everyday life.

Allocating Funds for Comfort: They might set aside a certain amount for enjoyable things (like nice meals or hobbies) rather than telling themselves they can never have any fun.

Maintaining a Savings Buffer: If possible, they like having a safety net in case of unexpected costs.

Preferring Steady Progress: Taurus is not usually the type to attempt extreme savings methods overnight. They would rather save a steady amount each month and watch it grow over time.

Because Taurus appreciates consistency, they might prefer budgeting tools or methods that are simple and predictable. They could keep track of expenses on paper, a spreadsheet, or a steady app that does not constantly change its features.

Saving Habits

Saving is often high on the Taurus priority list. They generally like the idea of having a financial cushion. Their saving habits might involve:

Automatic Transfers: Setting up a system where a portion of each paycheck goes straight into savings or an investment account. This way, they do not have to think about it every month.

Long-Term Perspective: Taurus might be comfortable leaving money in a savings account or a safe investment for years, knowing it will keep growing slowly.

Avoiding Unnecessary Risks: They often pick reliable savings vehicles, rather than chasing get-rich-quick schemes.

Saving for Specific Goals: Taurus might want to buy a home or a better car, or plan a special holiday. They can be patient about saving up until they have the funds to pay without anxiety.

One challenge is that if Taurus loves certain comforts, they could dip into their savings more often than intended. Balancing their enjoyment of small luxuries with the discipline to keep money set aside is key.

Spending Style

Taurus can be both careful and indulgent when it comes to spending. They often focus on quality over quantity. If they do buy something nice, they want it to last and be worth the cost. This can mean spending more upfront on a sturdy piece of furniture or quality shoes, believing it will pay off over the long run.

However, there are potential pitfalls:

Impulse Buying for Comfort: If Taurus feels stressed, they might soothe themselves by purchasing comfort items, like fancy snacks or cozy home goods. This can add up over time if not kept in check.

Reluctance to Spend: On the other hand, some Taurus individuals may become so cautious that they avoid spending even on things that could improve their lives.

Sticking to Familiar Brands: Taurus might remain loyal to the same shops or products, missing out on better deals or alternatives.

A balanced Taurus approach might involve researching products carefully, finding good value, and making sure that bigger purchases fit into their budget without causing sleepless nights.

Attitude Toward Debt

Debt can make Taurus uneasy because it threatens their sense of security. They usually prefer to keep debt as low as possible. If they must take on debt, like a mortgage, they want to be sure the payments are manageable.

Using Credit Wisely: Taurus might use credit cards for convenience but aim to pay the balance in full each month to avoid high interest.

Avoiding Loans for Luxury Items: They generally do not like the idea of borrowing money just to buy something fancy. Taurus would rather save first.

Paying Off Debts Slowly and Steadily: If they do have debts, they may set up a regular payment plan and stick to it until everything is cleared.

If a Taurus finds themselves in more debt than they are comfortable with, they might become anxious. In such cases, they can benefit from stepping back, listing out debts, and creating a practical plan to tackle them step by step.

Investing Preferences

When it comes to investing, Taurus often prefers lower-risk options. They like the idea of steady growth over time, rather than big ups and downs. This might include:

Savings Accounts or Certificates: Though these may have lower returns, they feel stable.

Bonds or Stable Funds: Taurus might lean toward investments known for dependability.

Property Investments: Some Taurus individuals like tangible assets, such as real estate, where they can see and manage the property.

Diverse Portfolios: They might spread money across a range of investments to avoid placing all their funds in one risky spot.

Because of their cautious nature, Taurus might sometimes miss out on higher returns from more daring investments. However, they value security more than the thrill of fast growth. They often want to see a proven record or have solid advice from a financial expert before venturing into new areas.

Luxury vs. Practicality

Many Taurus folks appreciate things that feel or look good—comfortable fabrics, well-made furniture, or tasty food. They might be willing to spend on items that elevate daily life. For them, it is not just spending money for the sake of it; it is about making their environment cozy.

But there is also a practical side in most Taurus personalities. They do not just want something because it is expensive; they want it to provide lasting value or an experience that truly enhances their life. For example, a Taurus might invest in a good mattress because they believe a good night's sleep is worth the cost, or they may buy quality cookware because it will last for many years.

Balancing these two sides—comfort and caution—can be tricky. Taurus might allow themselves a treat once in a while, but they generally want to know they are not destroying their budget in the process.

Sharing Finances with Others

When Taurus is in a household or relationship, money management can become more complex. Taurus usually likes to keep track of spending and might want to be sure that family members or partners are on the same page about budgeting. Some considerations include:

Joint Accounts: Taurus may or may not want a fully shared bank account. They might prefer a setup where household bills go into a joint account while maintaining some personal funds.

Clarity in Goals: Taurus wants to be sure everyone agrees on major expenses, like saving for a home or planning large purchases.

Regular Check-Ins: Sitting down monthly or quarterly to review spending can help avoid surprises.

Potential Conflict: If the partner or family member is a big spender or very impulsive, Taurus could feel uneasy. Communication is key to handle such differences.

Because Taurus values stability, they are likely to talk about money early in a relationship, making sure there are no big disagreements or hidden surprises that could shake their sense of security.

Money Worries and Stress

Taurus can become stressed if they feel money is not handled well, either by themselves or by people around them. Typical worries might include:

- **Unexpected Bills**: A sudden car repair or medical cost can throw them off balance.

- **Job Instability**: If they fear layoffs or company downsizing, they may feel anxious about the future.

- **Lack of Savings**: If they have not saved enough, they might experience more daily stress, worrying about each expense.

- **Family Expenses**: Children's needs, home repairs, or supporting relatives can increase pressure if there is no plan.

In times of stress, Taurus might need to revisit their budget, cut back on non-essentials for a while, or talk to someone they trust about financial planning. Taking practical steps usually helps them calm down.

Potential Pitfalls for Taurus and Money

No one is perfect with money, and Taurus is no exception. A few traps Taurus might fall into include:

Over-Spending on Comfort: If they are feeling down, a luxurious meal, plush home items, or fancy clothes might become too tempting. These small splurges can add up.

Fear of Investing: Their caution can keep them from growing their money in a balanced way. They might stick everything in low-interest accounts, missing better opportunities.

Stubbornness in Financial Habits: If someone suggests a new approach to saving or spending, Taurus might refuse to listen, saying, "What I do works fine," even if changes could help.

Overcommitting to a Purchase: Occasionally, Taurus might decide they want a big purchase (like a high-end car) and justify it by calling it an investment in comfort, while not fully considering the long-term financial strain.

By staying aware of these possibilities, Taurus can stop small money mistakes from growing into bigger issues.

Tips for Taurus to Manage Money Wisely

Create a Realistic Budget: Write down your monthly earnings and expenses, then set aside a portion for savings and a portion for enjoyment. Knowing you have some fun money can prevent sudden splurges.

Set Specific Goals: Whether it is buying a house, paying off debt, or funding an education, clear goals help you stay focused. Taurus does well when they see a goal as a practical mission.

Allow Small Treats: Cutting off all comforts might lead to frustration. Plan modest rewards so you do not feel deprived.

Compare Prices: Even if you prefer familiar brands, check other options. You might find similar quality at a lower cost.

Talk to Financial Advisors: Sometimes, professional advice on investments or retirement planning can help you balance security with growth.

Balance Now and Later: Remember that while it is wise to save for the future, enjoying the present is also valuable. Find a comfortable middle ground.

Practical Ways to Save Daily

Cooking at Home: Taurus often loves good food and can enjoy cooking meals that are both tasty and cheaper than eating out.

Buying in Bulk: For items you use regularly, buying larger quantities can save money.

Using Coupons or Deals: Some Taurus individuals are good at waiting for sales or looking for discounts, as long as it does not feel chaotic.

Energy Efficiency: Making small changes at home, like using efficient light bulbs or adjusting the thermostat, can help lower bills. Taurus might enjoy the idea of a stable, cozy home that is also cost-effective.

Long-Term Planning and Retirement

Taurus, with their steady nature, can be quite good at setting up long-term financial plans if they choose to focus on it. They might:

Open Retirement Accounts Early: Whether it is through an employer or a personal plan, they may start saving regularly.

Consider Real Estate: If they feel confident, buying property can appeal to their sense of stability.

Reinvest Earnings: If they do invest, they tend to keep it going, trusting the process of growth over many years.

Track Their Progress: Seeing the numbers rise slowly over time can give Taurus a sense of security.

If they ignore long-term planning, they might reach middle age or later and panic about having less saved than they would like. So, it is wise for Taurus to begin planning early, even if they start with small amounts.

Handling Money in Friendships and Family

Sharing money issues with friends or family can sometimes be stressful for Taurus, who values clarity and fairness. A few scenarios include:

Lending Money: Taurus can be generous, but they may worry about not getting repaid. They might prefer clear agreements rather than casual promises.

Splitting Bills: Taurus often wants a fair split. They can get annoyed if others are careless about who owes what.

Group Activities: If friends want to do expensive outings often, Taurus might feel pressured. They prefer to plan these events in advance, so they can budget accordingly.

Supporting Elderly Relatives: Taurus might plan carefully to assist older family members without risking their own savings.

Talking openly and setting boundaries can help Taurus avoid feeling taken advantage of. They might say something like, "I need to plan my expenses, so let's discuss this cost together before we move forward." This direct, calm approach fits their practical nature.

Teaching Money Skills to the Next Generation

If Taurus has children or younger relatives, they may enjoy passing on lessons about saving and spending. They can:

Give Small Allowances: Let kids learn how to divide money between saving and spending.

Show the Value of Work: Let them do small chores to earn a bit extra, teaching them that money can come from effort.

Encourage Simple Budgeting: For older children, they might create a mini-budget for school lunches or personal items.

Lead by Example: If Taurus parents manage money well, children see how calm planning leads to financial stability.

This can instill a sense of responsibility early on, which is something Taurus believes is important.

Staying Flexible

Taurus's preference for stability can sometimes cause them to be slow in adapting to changing financial times—like market shifts, new saving techniques, or digital payment methods. While caution is good, being too rigid can hold Taurus back. To stay flexible:

Review Budget Often: Prices and needs can change. Adjust your budget yearly or monthly as needed.

Explore Safely: If you want to try a new investment or saving method, start with a small amount to see how it goes.

Stay Informed: Read articles or watch simple finance tips to ensure you are not missing safer, more modern approaches.

Ask for Help: If you have a friend who is good with new money apps or digital banking, do not be afraid to learn from them.

Handling Unexpected Money Gains

Sometimes a Taurus might receive a bonus, inheritance, or other windfall. While it can be exciting, it also raises decisions about how to use that extra money. Taurus might:

- **Save Most of It**: Placing a good portion into savings or investments to secure their future.

- **Pay Off Debts**: If they have any debts, clearing them could be a relief.

- **Allow a Treat**: Taurus might pick one special item or experience. This satisfies their love of comfort without blowing the entire sum.

- **Plan Carefully**: They are likely to think about pros and cons before rushing to spend.

This cautious approach can help them avoid regrets and make the most of any sudden boost to their finances.

Recovering from Financial Setbacks

If Taurus experiences a job loss, unexpected debt, or other setback, they can feel shaken. But their patience and resilience can help them rebuild. Steps might include:

Assess the Damage: Taurus is good at looking at the numbers and seeing where things stand.

Cut Unneeded Costs: If times are tough, they can reduce non-essential spending until things improve.

Look for Stable Solutions: They might search for a new job or side gig that provides reliable income rather than high-risk ventures.

Seek Support: Talking with a trusted friend, family member, or professional can guide them toward realistic methods to bounce back.

Taurus often recovers because they will not give up easily. They value the comfort that comes from a secure financial base, so they will keep working toward that goal, step by step.

Combining Practicality and Enjoyment

Money management for Taurus is best when it includes both a strong practical side and room for enjoyment. If they never allow themselves any pleasant treats, they risk feeling frustrated. But if they spend on every appealing item, they may harm their savings. A middle approach might look like this:

Set Aside "Fun Money": Allocate a small portion of each paycheck for optional spending. No guilt, no worries.

Review Large Purchases: If thinking about buying something costly, give it a little time. Taurus can ask themselves, "Will I still want this in a month?" If yes, it might be worthwhile.

Celebrate Milestones Responsibly: When they reach a saving goal, they might do a modest, meaningful activity to enjoy that success in a measured way.

Stay Organized: Using budgeting apps or a simple journal to record incomes and expenses can help keep them on track.

By striking this balance, Taurus can keep financial stress low while still enjoying life's small pleasures.

CHAPTER 11: TAURUS AND OTHER SIGNS

Taurus is the second sign of the zodiac, but of course, it does not exist all by itself. The zodiac has twelve signs in total, and each sign has its own style, qualities, and challenges. When Taurus meets these other signs—whether as friends, family members, coworkers, or romantic partners—the two sides can feel harmony, tension, or a mix of both. In this chapter, we will explore how Taurus might interact with each of the other eleven signs and how these differences can be handled in a helpful way.

Please remember that what follows is just a general look. Real relationships depend on more than just sun signs. People have moon signs, rising signs, and personal life experiences that also shape who they are. Still, these broad ideas can show some patterns that come from combining Taurus traits with those of each other sign.

Taurus and Aries

Aries (March 21–April 19) is known for action, drive, and being the kind of sign that wants to start new things quickly. On the other hand, Taurus (April 20–May 20) tends to move at a slower pace, wanting to feel secure before changing anything. If you pair these signs, you might see:

Differences in Pace: Aries likes fast results; Taurus likes a steady approach. This can cause friction if Aries feels Taurus is too slow, or if Taurus feels Aries is too quick.

Shared Determination: Both Aries and Taurus can have a firm will. Aries is bold, while Taurus is steady. When they unite forces on a common goal, they can make real progress.

Handling Conflicts: An Aries might spark an argument, but Taurus prefers calm. If the topic is important, Taurus can dig in just as firmly as Aries. Each side has to practice patience.

To get along, Aries can learn that Taurus's careful thinking is useful, and Taurus can see that Aries's courage can open new doors.

Taurus and Gemini

Gemini (May 21–June 20) is known for curiosity, flexibility, and the urge to talk about many topics. Taurus, on the other hand, prefers consistency and might not enjoy too many changes at once.

Variety vs. Stability: Gemini might think Taurus is stubborn. Taurus might think Gemini is restless. But Gemini's quick mind can amuse Taurus if it does not push them to do things too differently all the time.

Communication Style: Gemini likes talking, bouncing between subjects. Taurus might speak less often but with deliberate focus. They can learn a lot from each other about sharing ideas in a calm yet interesting way.

Social Life: Gemini might enjoy meeting new people and exploring fresh events, while Taurus might prefer familiar hangouts. They can strike a balance by mixing new activities with comfortable routines.

When they find a middle ground, Taurus can help Gemini finish what they start, and Gemini can add fun sparks to Taurus's day.

Taurus and Cancer

Cancer (June 21–July 22) is often associated with warmth, home, and strong care for loved ones. Taurus values comfort and familiar environments. These two signs can find a natural connection.

Shared Love of Home: Both tend to seek a stable setting. Taurus loves physical comfort, while Cancer loves emotional comfort. They might enjoy cooking or quietly relaxing together.

Support System: Cancer is often known for caring gestures, and Taurus is known for loyalty. They can form a supportive bond where each one feels cared for.

Moody vs. Steady: Cancer can be more changeable in mood. Taurus, being more even-keeled, might help keep Cancer steady. At the same time, Taurus must be mindful of Cancer's need for emotional understanding.

In friendships or family ties, they can blend very well if they respect each other's calm side and emotional side.

Taurus and Leo

Leo (July 23–August 22) is proud, likes to stand out, and often wants admiration. Taurus is calmer, more private about seeking recognition. These signs can clash or bond, depending on how they handle each other's differences.

Desire for Appreciation: Leo wants attention and praise, while Taurus might prefer quiet affirmation. If Taurus forgets to acknowledge Leo's efforts, Leo can feel neglected. At the same time, Leo should recognize Taurus's need for reassurance in a calmer way.

Enjoyment of Comfort and Good Times: Leo enjoys grand parties and flashy fun, while Taurus prefers smaller but pleasant gatherings.

Still, both can share a taste for well-made items, like quality clothes or furniture, though Leo might prefer bolder styles.

Stubborn vs. Proud: Both are fixed signs. Taurus can be inflexible in routines, and Leo can be inflexible in personal pride. They must practice compromise so neither side always insists on having things their way.

With mutual respect, they can form a strong pair: Taurus provides steadiness, Leo brings cheerful leadership.

Taurus and Virgo

Virgo (August 23–September 22) shares the earth element with Taurus. Both signs tend to be practical, grounded, and thoughtful about everyday tasks.

Common Practicality: Both like a well-organized life. Virgo might pay a lot of attention to details, while Taurus methodically works through a plan. They can make a smooth team if they split tasks according to each other's skills.

Different Worries: Virgo can get anxious over small problems, while Taurus might feel that some details are not worth stressing about. Taurus's calm might soothe Virgo, and Virgo's thoroughness can prevent Taurus from overlooking small but important issues.

Shared Reliability: They can trust each other. If they promise to show up at a set time, they likely will.

This pairing can be strong in any context—family, friendship, or work—because of mutual respect for steady, careful ways.

Taurus and Libra

Libra (September 23–October 22) is also ruled by Venus, the same planet that rules Taurus. But Libra is an air sign, while Taurus is an earth sign, so they display this Venus influence in different ways.

Harmony vs. Stability: Libra loves balance and might talk about fairness or beauty in ideas, while Taurus focuses on comfort and the physical side of things. They share an interest in aesthetics but approach it in distinct ways.

Cooperative Spirit: Libra wants to keep everyone happy, while Taurus wants to keep things calm. Often, these goals align. They can enjoy art, nice food, and a harmonious social setting together.

Indecisiveness vs. Firmness: Libra might struggle to pick a side, aiming to please everyone. Taurus can offer a grounded stance, although if Taurus becomes stubborn, Libra might feel overshadowed.

With open communication, Taurus's reliability combines well with Libra's charm. Each can learn how to approach problems with both warmth and practical sense.

Taurus and Scorpio

Scorpio (October 23–November 21) is the opposite sign of Taurus in the zodiac wheel. Opposite does not necessarily mean conflict. Often, it means these two can learn a lot from each other, but they must handle differences carefully.

Shared Fixed Nature: Both are fixed signs, which means they are persistent and can resist change. If they agree on a goal, they can be unstoppable. If they disagree, they can both become unyielding.

Emotional Depth vs. Practical Calm: Scorpio feels things very deeply and may want to explore hidden motivations. Taurus is more direct and focuses on real-world actions. Scorpio might see Taurus as not probing enough, while Taurus might see Scorpio as overly intense.

Trust and Loyalty: Each can be very loyal. Scorpio wants emotional loyalty; Taurus wants reliability and honesty. If they build trust, this bond can feel very strong.

To get along, they should respect each other's ways of dealing with life's challenges. Taurus can offer stability, while Scorpio can help Taurus explore deeper emotions.

Taurus and Sagittarius

Sagittarius (November 22–December 21) is known for a love of discovery and new experiences. Taurus, however, likes the familiar path and might hesitate to accept big changes without a plan.

Different Focus: Sagittarius is often excited by ideas or travel. Taurus focuses on daily life and physical comfort. They can clash if Sagittarius's free spirit feels boxed in, or if Taurus feels pushed out of a stable routine.

Teaching Each Other: If they try, Taurus can help Sagittarius stay grounded and plan carefully. Meanwhile, Sagittarius can encourage Taurus to be open to new possibilities.

Patience and Fun: Sagittarius might crack jokes or spontaneously suggest an outing. Taurus might need a bit of time to decide. Balancing spontaneity with predictability is key.

When they find middle ground, they can enjoy each other's style. Sagittarius can bring an energetic spark to Taurus's life, while Taurus offers a calm, reliable base.

Taurus and Capricorn

Capricorn (December 22–January 19) is another earth sign, which usually means a natural fit with Taurus. Both are practical, patient, and focused on concrete achievements.

Long-Term Goals: Capricorn often aims high in work or personal plans. Taurus understands the need to build something step by step. Together, they can form a strong team if they share a vision.

Methodical Approach: Both like to plan. Taurus is steady in routine, while Capricorn is strategic about climbing to success. They might approach tasks in a slow but sure way, making real progress over time.

Possible Challenge: Capricorn can become too serious or work-focused. Taurus loves comfort and might remind Capricorn to relax. On the other hand, Taurus might become complacent, and Capricorn can push them to do more.

These signs can create a stable bond based on trust, shared values, and the willingness to take one step after another until they reach their goals.

Taurus and Aquarius

Aquarius (January 20–February 18) is an air sign known for forward-thinking ideas and a desire to break away from too much tradition. Taurus is an earth sign that tends to stick with tried-and-true ways.

Different Visions: Aquarius might discuss big plans for society or the future, while Taurus wants real proof that something works. They can butt heads if Aquarius sees Taurus as closed-minded, or if Taurus sees Aquarius as unrealistic.

Shared Persistence: Both are fixed signs, so they can each be stubborn, just in different ways. If they focus on a shared goal, Taurus can ground Aquarius's big ideas in tangible steps, and Aquarius can expand Taurus's limited viewpoint.

Social vs. Private: Aquarius often likes group gatherings or community-related pursuits, while Taurus might prefer a smaller circle. They can learn from each other's social styles if they remain respectful.

Finding a balance between stable methods and creative visions can help them form a relationship that blends practicality with innovation.

Taurus and Pisces

Pisces (February 19–March 20) is a water sign that can be dreamy, empathic, and sometimes quiet. Taurus, while more grounded in the physical realm, can connect with Pisces if they share a gentle approach.

Calm Environment: Both can value peace. Taurus wants a relaxed setting, and Pisces often avoids harsh conflict. They might enjoy calm pastimes, like reading, watching soothing shows, or creating art.

Balancing Feelings and Reality: Pisces can get lost in daydreams. Taurus can help bring practical structure to those ideas. In return, Pisces can help Taurus be more sensitive to emotional or creative sides.

Possible Pitfalls: If Pisces is too indecisive or easily swayed, Taurus might feel frustrated. Pisces might see Taurus as too rigid. But with kind support, they can understand each other's habits and find harmony.

This pair can build a gentle, warm connection, mixing Taurus's steady presence with Pisces's imaginative spirit.

General Observations

When looking at Taurus with any other sign, certain patterns tend to come up:

Patience Helps: Taurus does best with people who understand that they work and think at a calm pace. Signs that move quickly can still get along with Taurus by showing understanding and explaining new ideas clearly.

Respect for Boundaries: Taurus wants to feel safe. Any sign that bullies Taurus into changes, or who teases them constantly, risks pushing Taurus away. On the other hand, if Taurus never tries to bend, they might frustrate more flexible signs.

Mutual Benefit: Taurus is loyal and reliable, which many signs appreciate. In turn, Taurus can learn from signs that bring new ideas or emotional insights.

Clear Communication: If there is a big difference in pace or style, it helps to talk honestly about it. Taurus may not enjoy big debates, but open conversations can clear misunderstandings before they turn into major issues.

Tips for Taurus Getting Along with Any Sign

Stay Open: Even if you like routine, give others a chance to share their perspective. You might discover useful methods or fun activities.

Explain Your Needs: Let friends, family, or coworkers know you prefer a clear plan or schedule. That way, they can avoid springing surprises on you.

Learn Basic Differences: If you know your friend is a fire sign who thrives on quick actions, try to adapt at times. Also, kindly ask them to let you prepare.

Build Patience for Opposites: Opposite signs (like Scorpio) or signs with very different styles (like Gemini or Aquarius) can teach you a lot if you stay patient.

Find Shared Ground: Many signs share at least one interest with you. If you both like good food, music, or a certain craft, use that as a positive bridge.

Tips for Other Signs Working with Taurus

Present Change Gradually: Taurus is more willing to adapt if they see the benefits and have some time to think.

Offer Consistency: Try to keep your word. If you say you will be there at a certain time, make an effort to show up. Taurus values trust deeply.

Show Real Appreciation: Taurus might not seek praise loudly, but a sincere note or comment recognizing their effort can go a long way.

Avoid Pushing Too Hard: If you force Taurus to act fast, they might dig in. Instead, calmly explain why quick action is needed and how it can help everyone.

Respect Their Need for a Steady Base: Let Taurus have their zone of comfort, whether it's a favorite seat at home or a certain routine at work.

Cooperation in Groups

In group settings with multiple signs, Taurus can be an anchor. They may help others stay on track. However, if the group is made up of very spontaneous signs, they might find Taurus's caution a bit slow. By learning to keep an open mind, Taurus can hold onto their strong suits (like planning and patience) while still letting others bring creative or fast-paced energy. The result can be a balanced group that gets things done without needless disorder.

Friendships Across Signs

Fire Signs (Aries, Leo, Sagittarius): Can add excitement, inspire Taurus to explore new hobbies, and lighten the mood. Taurus can offer them support and a down-to-earth viewpoint.

Air Signs (Gemini, Libra, Aquarius): Bring fresh ideas and spark conversations. Taurus can give them practicality, turning lofty plans into results.

Water Signs (Cancer, Scorpio, Pisces): Blend well with Taurus's calm nature, offering emotional warmth. Taurus provides them with stability, while water signs share deeper feelings.

Earth Signs (Virgo, Capricorn): Share a similar grounded approach. This can lead to mutual respect and easier cooperation.

Friendships flourish when both sides accept each other's ways without trying to force big changes all the time.

Romantic Relationships Across Signs

Romance can be complex, but a few things often stand out with Taurus:

Taurus and Fire: Sparks can fly. Fire signs bring excitement, Taurus brings steadiness. They must handle the difference in pace.

Taurus and Air: Air signs keep the relationship interesting mentally, while Taurus keeps it grounded. They must talk about plans and changes clearly.

Taurus and Water: Can be a soothing mix, though they need to watch for emotional storms if the water sign is very sensitive.

Taurus and Earth: Usually an easy bond, though they risk getting stuck if both become too fixed in routines.

Trust and kindness can handle most differences, but it is helpful if each person understands the other's style and respects it.

Resolving Differences in a Taurus-Mixed Household

Families can include many zodiac signs. If Taurus is living with signs that like to change things often, it may be wise to:

Plan Adjustments: Let Taurus know about major changes (like rearranging a room or planning a big event) in advance.

Respect Quiet Areas: If Taurus needs a calm corner, especially in a busy family, that can help them recharge.

Divide Chores: Taurus is good at tasks that need patience, like cooking carefully or tending to the garden, while more energetic signs can take on jobs that need speed.

Hold Family Check-Ins: A brief talk about weekly schedules can help avoid surprising Taurus with sudden events.

Appreciating Differences Without Judgment

One of the best things about mixing signs is that they can balance each other. Taurus benefits from the lively energy of some signs, the deep emotions of others, and the new ideas of the rest. Meanwhile, those signs benefit from Taurus's consistency. The main risk is when each side clings too tightly to its own style and will not listen. Patience, open minds, and a willingness to step outside one's comfort zone occasionally can do wonders for bridging these gaps.

CHAPTER 12: CARING FOR YOURSELF AS A TAURUS

Being a Taurus often means you have a calm, reliable style and a deep need for security and comfort. But caring for yourself goes beyond just enjoying soft blankets or good food. It also means managing stress in healthy ways, paying attention to your physical and mental well-being, and making sure you do not get trapped by stubborn routines. In this chapter, we will look at what self-care means for Taurus, covering physical habits, emotional balance, personal growth, and strategies to avoid burnout.

Why Self-Care Matters for Taurus

All zodiac signs benefit from looking after themselves, but Taurus might find it especially important because:

Physical Comfort Is Key: Taurus often loves restful surroundings, which can be good for relaxation but may lead to too much inactivity if taken too far.

Stress Affects Stability: If Taurus feels rushed or sees their routines shaken up, it can cause anxiety. Proper self-care helps them stay composed.

Preference for Routine: Regular self-care habits fit well with Taurus's love of structure, but it also means they have to watch out for boredom or rigid patterns.

Steady Energy: Taurus can persist for a long time, working or caring for others, but eventually, they might get drained if they do not remember to rest and refresh.

When Taurus invests time in healthy habits and emotional awareness, they can enjoy life more and keep their strong, calm nature intact.

Building a Calm Environment

Because Taurus connects with the earth and likes to feel at ease, the place where they live or spend their most personal moments can shape their mood a lot. Here are some ways to create a soothing space:

Choose Relaxing Colors: Earthy tones or gentle shades can help Taurus feel settled.

Comfortable Furniture: A supportive bed, a cozy chair, or a tidy desk can all help. Taurus might splurge on a quality mattress or a strong piece of furniture that lasts.
Natural Elements: Plants, fresh flowers, or even a small indoor herb area can connect Taurus to nature. Opening a window for fresh air can also bring calm.
Organized Space: A clutter-free environment can keep the mind clear. Taurus often likes to know where everything is, so neat storage or labeled boxes may help.

A relaxed home environment does not have to be fancy. It just needs to feel secure and comfortable.

Physical Well-Being

Taurus is an earth sign with a strong link to the body. Paying attention to physical health is crucial. Some pointers:

Consistent Sleep: Taurus thrives on routine, and that includes bedtime. Going to bed and waking up at similar times can give the body the rest it needs.

Balanced Diet: Taurus often enjoys good food, but that can lead to overeating if not watched. A well-rounded diet with occasional treats can satisfy their senses without harming health.

Gentle Exercise: While some Taurus individuals might prefer calm walks or simple stretching, moderate regular activity helps maintain strength and reduce stress. Overly intense workouts might feel harsh, so a comfortable pace often works better.

Avoiding Lethargy: Because Taurus likes comfort, there is a risk of sitting too long. Getting up for short breaks to move around can protect against stiffness and low energy.

By mixing steady exercise, restful sleep, and mindful eating, Taurus can keep their body strong without feeling forced into extreme regimes.

Emotional Health and Handling Stress

Even though Taurus is often calm, they do feel stress, especially if routines break down or if they sense financial or personal insecurity. Ways to maintain emotional balance:

Planned Downtime: Set aside blocks of quiet time for reading, drawing, meditating, or any calming hobby. This helps avoid overload.

Breathing Techniques: Slow, deep breaths can help calm the mind. Taurus might find it easy to develop a steady breathing habit because they like consistent rhythms.

Talking with Trusted People: Taurus may be private, but opening up to a close friend or counselor can prevent bottled-up feelings.

Engaging the Senses: Listening to soothing music, lighting a lightly scented candle, or relaxing with gentle background sounds can reduce tension.

Whenever stress hits, Taurus can remind themselves that they do not have to fix everything at once. Step-by-step solutions work well for them.

Setting Healthy Boundaries

Taurus tends to be loyal and might sometimes say "yes" more than they should, trying to keep peace. Learning to set boundaries can guard their well-being:

Know Personal Limits: If asked to stay late at work or attend events daily, Taurus should check how this fits with their need for rest.

Practice Polite Refusals: Saying "I would love to help, but I can't take on more right now" can keep relationships smooth while still protecting personal energy.

Plan Alone Time: Taurus needs periods of quiet to recharge. Putting "private time" on the schedule helps prevent others from assuming they are always free.

Speak Up Early: If something feels unfair, addressing it calmly can prevent bigger issues later.

Good boundaries do not mean shutting out others. They just mean finding a balance between giving and keeping enough space for oneself.

Avoiding Ruts in Routine

A big challenge for Taurus is the risk of getting stuck in old habits. Though routines make them feel safe, repeating the same pattern for too long might block growth or lead to boredom. Here are ways Taurus can break out gently:

Small Experiments: Try a new recipe, a different walking route, or a short online class. Tiny changes can freshen the routine without feeling overwhelming.

Scheduled Variety: Maybe once a month, do something out of the ordinary—visit a museum, try a different hobby, or rearrange a part of the home.

Team Up: If it helps, do it with a friend who enjoys trying new things. That social aspect might ease Taurus's nerves about change.

Reward System: For every small new step, Taurus can allow a bit of comfort afterward, like a nice cup of tea. This encourages them to keep going.

Embracing a little novelty can bring new energy and ideas, keeping Taurus from feeling stuck.

Managing Stubborn Streaks

Taurus is known for being stubborn. Sometimes that helps—like when finishing a difficult task—but it can also hold them back when it prevents them from listening to feedback. Some ways to handle stubbornness:

Pause Before Refusal: When someone suggests a change or a different opinion, hold off on saying "no" immediately. Give it a day or two.

Find Common Ground: If a new idea feels too big, see if there's a smaller version that feels safer.

Use Logical Lists: Writing pros and cons can help Taurus see if a suggestion makes sense. This method appeals to their practical side.

Ask for Explanation: Sometimes, Taurus resists because they do not understand the benefits. Encouraging others to clarify can open the door to acceptance.

Being open does not mean losing one's identity; it just means giving new thoughts a fair chance.

Hobbies That May Suit Taurus

Self-care also means finding activities that bring genuine pleasure or relaxation. Some hobbies that can fit Taurus's earthy and patient nature include:

Gardening: Connecting with the earth can feel grounding. Watching plants grow slowly is a natural fit for Taurus.

Cooking or Baking: Taurus often likes using the senses, and cooking lets them enjoy textures, flavors, and aromas.

Painting or Crafts: Quiet, hands-on activities can be soothing, allowing Taurus to see steady progress in their creations.

Reading or Audiobooks: Engaging the mind in a calm setting. Taurus might enjoy stories that are easy to follow or practical books on subjects that interest them.

Collecting or Organizing: If they enjoy certain items, like stamps or coins, collecting can tap into their liking for structure and beauty.

Of course, Taurus can pick any hobby they like, but these are a few that match their natural style.

Building Supportive Relationships

Taking care of yourself often means making sure you have a social circle that respects your need for calm and reliability:

Choosing Trustworthy Friends: Taurus does not need a large group, but rather a circle of people who are dependable, kind, and understanding.

Communicating Needs: If you need quiet evenings or gentle conversation, let friends know. This prevents them from mistaking your calmness for disinterest.

Giving Back: Taurus's loyalty is a precious gift to friends. By offering genuine support when they need it, you strengthen bonds.

Watching Out for Energy Drains: If someone constantly brings chaos or guilt, it might be wise to keep some distance. Protecting your calm atmosphere is part of self-care.

A balanced circle helps Taurus feel secure without feeling smothered by too many commitments.

Mindful Spending for Comfort

We have discussed finances in a previous chapter, but it is worth touching on how money ties in with self-care for Taurus. Since Taurus likes comfort, a few tips:

Set a Comfort Budget: Decide how much you can spend on small treats each month without harming your larger goals.

Pick Quality Over Quantity: Buy one well-made sweater instead of several cheap ones that wear out quickly. This suits Taurus's preference for lasting value.

Try Thrifting or Secondhand: Good deals on sturdy items can be found, which means you do not have to overspend to feel comfortable.

Save for Special Items: If there is a bigger purchase that would really add to your quality of life, plan for it steadily. The wait can make it feel more rewarding.

By staying conscious of spending, Taurus can indulge in comfort while keeping a stable financial base.

Keeping Goals Flexible

Taurus is great at sticking to a plan, but that plan might sometimes become too rigid. To practice healthy self-care, Taurus can:

Check-In Regularly: Every few months, review your goals. Are they still meaningful to you?

Adjust When Needed: If life changes, do not be afraid to shift course. This does not mean you failed; it means you are adapting.

Celebrate Small Successes: A small success is worth noting, like finishing a difficult project or making steady progress on a new skill.

Stay Open to New Ideas: Sometimes a better path appears. Being willing to adjust prevents frustration later.

Allowing some flexibility keeps Taurus from feeling trapped or disappointed if circumstances shift.

Handling Emotional Ups and Downs

While Taurus might not display their emotions as openly as some signs, they still feel things deeply. Ignoring emotions can lead to surprise outbursts or stored resentment. A few methods to keep emotional health in check:

Journaling: Writing thoughts at the end of the day can help process worries or joys in a quiet, private way.

Gentle Self-Talk: Instead of pushing yourself to "just get over it," try to speak kindly to yourself. Example: "I am feeling upset, and it is okay to take a moment to breathe."

Slow, Steady Processing: If a situation at work or with friends bothers you, do not hide it forever. Take time to calm down, then talk about it with someone you trust or address it directly if needed.

Relaxation Techniques: Activities like gentle yoga, a warm bath, or a quiet time in nature can let you unwind at your own pace.

This approach helps Taurus remain calm on the surface while also handling deeper feelings in a healthy manner.

Connecting with Nature

Taurus, as an earth sign, can find great relief in connecting with the natural world. Ideas for nurturing this link:

Walks or Hikes: Even a short stroll in a local park can ground you.

Gardening: Growing herbs or flowers can be therapeutic, and watching the slow process of growth matches Taurus's patient style.

Open-Air Activities: Picnics, gentle outdoor games, or simply reading outside can help Taurus breathe fresh air and feel physically relaxed.

Observing Seasonal Changes: Notice how the environment shifts across different times of the year. This can remind Taurus that life does include cycles of change, but many of them happen steadily.

Nature can soothe Taurus's mind and offer perspective that change does not have to be sudden or scary.

Practical Approaches to Relaxation

Taurus might not always like long or complicated meditation routines, but simpler methods can be quite effective:

Senses Check: Pause and notice what you see, hear, smell, taste, and feel. This brief grounding practice can center you.

Progressive Muscle Relaxation: Tense and relax muscle groups one by one, moving from toes to head. This can relieve physical tension.

Guided Imagery: Imagine a calm place or scenario that feels peaceful and safe—like a favorite beach or a quiet forest. This can help reduce stress.

Slow Routine Tasks: For example, washing dishes or folding laundry with mindful attention can become a steadying activity, letting you move at a careful pace.

Taurus's natural patience means these steady, methodical practices can feel comforting rather than boring.

Letting Go of What No Longer Serves You

Because Taurus can be sentimental or hold onto things for comfort, it is important to learn when to let go. This can apply to old possessions, stale routines, or even negative patterns.

Decluttering: Removing items you no longer use can make your space lighter and your mind clearer. Doing this gradually can feel less overwhelming.

Ending Unhelpful Patterns: Maybe you realize a nightly habit is harming your sleep. Changing that habit can improve your overall well-being.

Releasing Past Grudges: Taurus sometimes holds onto old hurts. Talking with someone, writing a letter you never send, or seeking professional advice can help you free yourself from lingering anger.

Shedding what no longer fits your life opens space for healthier routines and better items or habits.

Balancing Work and Personal Life

As discussed earlier, Taurus works steadily. However, too much focus on work can drain their love for life:

Clear Stop Times: Decide when you will end your workday. This helps ensure you have downtime for yourself.

Free Days: If possible, keep at least one day a week mostly unscheduled. This day can be used for rest, gentle hobbies, or seeing friends at a calm pace.

Check Work Stress: If your job feels too chaotic, see if there are small ways to reorganize tasks or talk to a supervisor. Taurus thrives with order and consistency.

Rewarding Routines: Plan something soothing after a busy day, like a warm shower or reading time. Knowing a treat is waiting can lower stress.

Striking a balanced pace makes it more likely you will stay both productive and content.

Positive Self-Talk and Affirmations

While Taurus can be confident, they might also slip into negative self-talk if shaken. Simple affirmations or reminders can help:

- **"I move at my own steady pace, and that is okay."**
- **"I deserve moments of rest and comfort."**
- **"It is all right to change plans if I see a better way."**
- **"I trust my ability to handle problems one step at a time."**

Such reminders do not have to be loud or dramatic. They can simply be gentle thoughts that keep Taurus grounded when doubts arise.

Professional Guidance

Sometimes, Taurus might benefit from talking to a counselor or therapist. This can be especially true if they have trouble adjusting to a big life change or if they are storing too much stress. A therapist who respects Taurus's need for a calm approach can guide them in learning new coping methods without pushing them too fast. Taurus might initially be reserved, but with time, they can find these talks very helpful for emotional well-being.

Creating a Self-Care Checklist

Making a self-care checklist can keep Taurus on track, appealing to their preference for clear routines. It might include:

- **Morning**: Drink water, stretch for five minutes, check a simple to-do list.

- **Midday**: Pause for a few calming breaths, eat a balanced meal, walk or stand for a couple of minutes.

- **Evening**: Tidy a small area, note something you are thankful for, enjoy a quiet hobby or relaxing music.

- **Weekly**: Plan one fun or restful activity, prepare an easy meal you like, and review your finances briefly to avoid surprises.

Adjust these steps to fit personal needs. Checking them off might feel satisfying, and small daily efforts can add up.

CHAPTER 13: TAURUS AND DAILY HABITS

A day is made up of many small actions, from the moment you open your eyes to when you go to sleep at night. For a Taurus, these little routines can hold special meaning because they often find safety in knowing what to expect. For example, having a predictable morning wake-up time or a favorite place to sit for breakfast can bring a sense of calm. At the same time, a Taurus can sometimes get stuck if each day follows the exact pattern without any room for change. Balancing consistency with openness can help a Taurus shape daily habits that feel both comforting and refreshing.

In this chapter, we will look at how a Taurus might handle different parts of the day—from morning tasks to nighttime wind-down routines—and consider ways to build healthy habits without becoming too rigid. We will also consider how to respond to sudden changes in your daily schedule, so that a Taurus can remain steady even when life throws a curve.

The Value of Daily Habits for Taurus

For many Taurus individuals, daily habits are not just chores or tasks—they are anchors. Predictable actions, such as brushing your teeth at a certain time or having a regular breakfast, can keep you feeling secure. Having a plan for the day ahead can lower stress because you know what is coming. Instead of worrying about everything at once, you can focus on one step at a time.

But daily habits also help Taurus do well at tasks. Because Taurus is patient and likes to move step by step, a solid routine can prevent them from feeling rushed. For instance, if a Taurus has a steady morning practice of making a simple to-do list, it ensures they do not forget important responsibilities. With these small, reliable steps, Taurus can maintain a calm pace that matches their steady nature.

However, it is wise to remember that routines can become dull if there is never any variety. Too much predictability might mean missing chances to try new things. This chapter will talk about how to find a middle ground: enjoying a routine while keeping an open mind to small differences that can add sparkle to each day.

Morning Routines for a Grounded Start

Many people say the morning sets the tone for the rest of the day. For a Taurus, having a gentle but reliable morning routine can be especially helpful. Here are some ideas that might suit a Taurus's style:

Wake Up Gently
 Taurus might prefer a calm start to the day rather than a loud alarm. Choosing a softer sound or a gentle piece of music can ease you out of sleep more kindly.

Brief Stretch or Light Movement
 Taurus often appreciates physical comfort, but it is also important to prepare the body for the day. A little stretching or a short walk outside can help your muscles wake up. It does not have to be intense—just enough to loosen any stiffness.

A Consistent Breakfast
 Having a tasty and balanced breakfast can nourish both body and mind. Taurus might pick something hearty, like oatmeal with fruit or a simple egg dish. A familiar breakfast can be comforting, though occasionally trying a new recipe might spark some variety.

Planning the Day

Before diving into any activities, a Taurus may benefit from writing down a short list of tasks for the day. This helps keep track of responsibilities and sets a direction. Since Taurus can handle tasks one by one, a daily list can be more helpful than a huge monthly plan.

Calm, Unhurried Pace

Rushing can make Taurus feel stressed. Waking up early enough to avoid a chaotic scramble sets a peaceful tone. If you prefer to sleep longer, you can plan for a streamlined morning routine, but be sure it still includes a moment or two of quiet.

Midday Habits and Work Breaks

Moving into midday, Taurus may find themselves at work or handling daily errands. Whether in an office, at home, or out in the field, certain habits can keep them focused and steady:

Scheduled Breaks

Taurus thrives on pacing themselves. Rather than pushing nonstop until exhaustion, plan small pauses to rest your mind. For instance, take five minutes every couple of hours to stand, stretch, or sip water. This routine can fight fatigue and boost concentration.

Purposeful Lunch

A Taurus often enjoys meals and may look forward to lunchtime. Instead of grabbing something random, planning lunch in advance can be more relaxing. If you bring food from home, choose satisfying, nutritious options. If you prefer to buy lunch, picking a spot with reliable favorites can lower stress.

Physical Comfort at Work

Because Taurus is sensitive to their environment, paying attention to ergonomics can help. Make sure your chair is supportive, the computer screen is at a good height, and your workspace feels calm. A small plant or a pleasing photograph can add to the sense of comfort.

Steady Progress on Tasks
Taurus likes to finish one thing before moving on. Try breaking big tasks into smaller steps, checking them off one by one. This approach fits the Taurus love of order and can keep tasks from feeling overwhelming.

Small Spontaneous Choices
Adding a small twist to your midday routine—like walking a slightly different path back to your workstation or trying a new fruit for dessert—can give a bit of freshness without shaking your overall structure.

Afternoon Energy Slumps and How to Manage Them

Many people experience a dip in energy in the early to mid-afternoon. For Taurus, who may already enjoy a slower pace, this slump can feel extra heavy. Here are some suggestions:

Short Walk or Light Stretch
If you can, step outside for a brief walk. Fresh air and mild movement can recharge you. Even a walk around the building can refresh your mind.

Healthy Hydration
Drinking enough water or herbal tea can keep your energy from dropping too low. Sugary drinks might give a quick rush, but they often lead to a crash later.

Gentle Snacks
If your stomach is growling and mealtime is far away, a small snack—like nuts, a piece of cheese, or fruit—can help stabilize

energy. Taurus might enjoy nibbling on something with a nice taste or texture, but take care not to go overboard with snacking to avoid feeling sluggish.

Task Switching
If possible, switch to a different type of task for a short time. For instance, if you have been answering emails all morning, try doing something more hands-on or creative in the afternoon. A change in mental focus can break through monotony.

Mindful Rest
Some people find a quick rest break helpful. Even leaning back in your chair with your eyes closed for a few moments can calm the mind. However, be careful not to doze off if that is not allowed in your setting.

Evening Wind-Down Routine

When the day is done and it is time to head home, Taurus often looks forward to unwinding. Even if you work from home, having a clear transition from "work mode" to "personal time" can help you relax:

Slow Shift from Work
If you commute, consider playing soothing music or an enjoyable audiobook on the ride. If you work at home, try tidying your workspace before stepping away. This draws a line between work tasks and personal space.

Comfort at Dinner
Taurus might relish a tasty, comforting meal. However, watch portion sizes and heavy foods if they make you too sleepy or weigh you down. A balanced dinner with some fresh vegetables can be both delicious and helpful for your body.

Relaxing Activities
 An evening hobby that lowers stress—like reading a simple book, coloring, or working on a puzzle—can give your mind a break. If you prefer more social time, a calm conversation or gentle board game can also be pleasant.

Lowering Lights
 As bedtime approaches, dimming household lights can signal your brain to get ready for rest. Taurus is sensitive to environment, so a soft lamp or warm glow can set a cozy mood.

Unplug Before Sleep
 Bright screens or intense news stories may wind you up at night. Switching off devices or putting them aside at least 30 minutes before bed can promote more restful sleep. Instead, you might sip a mild herbal tea or do a few simple stretches.

Weekend Habits and Personal Projects

For Taurus, weekends or days off can be prime time for deeper rest and practical errands. Yet it is also a chance to explore interests outside of your usual routine, if you allow a bit of variety:

Routine vs. Exploration
 If you always spend your free days in the same way—like staying in bed late and then doing chores—try adding a small new element, such as visiting a local market or attempting a home project you have never done before.

Physical Creativity
 Taurus often has a knack for craft or gardening. Devoting part of your weekend to making something with your hands can be calming and fulfilling. It might be painting a small furniture piece, repotting plants, or baking bread.

Social but Calm

If you want to see friends, pick a setting that feels relaxed. A brunch or a slow-paced outdoor meetup might be more appealing than a loud, crowded place.

Household Tasks

Many people do errands or clean on days off. For Taurus, turning these tasks into a peaceful routine—like playing quiet music while folding laundry—can keep you from feeling rushed. This methodical approach can make chores almost soothing.

Self-Care Appointments

If needed, schedule time for personal well-being. This might be a haircut, a gentle spa treatment, or a check-in with a therapist if you find it beneficial. Making the appointment part of your weekend can keep it from getting lost in the workweek chaos.

Adjusting to Sudden Changes

One challenge for Taurus is dealing with unexpected alterations to the daily schedule. Life is not always predictable, and sometimes you have to adapt quickly:

Stay Calm First

When a sudden change happens—like a canceled appointment or a traffic jam—take a few slow breaths. Recognize that even if the schedule is thrown off, you can still manage your day.

Look for Simple Solutions

If a meeting is canceled, maybe you can use that time to complete a task you were putting off. If traffic is bad, maybe call ahead to let people know you will be late, reducing stress.

Keep a Basic Backup Plan
Taurus can benefit from having a small "emergency kit" for daily life. For instance, keep a snack in your bag or phone charger with you so that small disruptions do not become big problems.

Seek Help if Needed
If the change is big (like a major project shift at work), do not be afraid to speak with colleagues or a manager for guidance. Taurus is reliable, but that does not mean you must handle every shift alone.

Recover and Reflect
After the unexpected event, a Taurus might feel unsettled. Spend a bit of time reviewing what happened and how you handled it. Next time, you will be more prepared for quick changes.

Balancing Steady Habits with Spontaneity

Routines are good for Taurus, but too much sameness can sometimes lead to a dull feeling. Adding small bursts of spontaneity can keep your mind active without causing stress:

Gentle Changes
Instead of changing everything at once, pick small details to vary, like trying a different route on a walk or wearing a color you normally do not choose.

Keep a List of New Ideas
You might write down interesting local spots, recipes, or crafts you want to try someday. When you feel open to something different, pick one from the list.

Support from Friends
If you have a friend who enjoys planning small adventures, let them suggest an outing once a month. Make sure it is not too high-pressure or too far outside your comfort zone.

One New Habit at a Time

If you want to add variety to your daily routine, do so step by step. For example, if you decide to walk for 15 minutes in the morning, focus on that for a couple of weeks before adding another new habit.

Rewards After New Experiences

If trying something new makes you nervous, treat yourself with something comforting afterwards—like reading a calming chapter of a book or sipping a favorite tea. This can help you feel that even a small shift in routine ends on a comfortable note.

Handling Time Wasters and Distractions

While Taurus appreciates a steady pace, it is easy to slip into unproductive habits, such as spending too much time scrolling on a phone or getting lost in daydreams. Here are some ways to keep distractions in check:

Set Boundaries with Devices

Decide on specific times or durations for checking social media. Taurus might do well with a set schedule—like 15 minutes in the morning or after lunch—so that phone time does not interrupt the entire day.

Plan Relaxation Moments

If you feel the urge to distract yourself, it might mean you need a real break. Plan short rests that let you zone out in a healthy way, such as listening to soothing music or gazing out the window.

Keep Tasks Visible

Taurus does well when reminded of practical tasks. A physical or digital to-do list can gently push you to return to tasks when you notice you are drifting into idle activities.

Create a Comfortable Work Setting
Sometimes distractions occur because your workspace feels unpleasant. If you adjust the lighting, temperature, or seating, you might be less tempted to wander off from boredom or discomfort.

Reward Yourself After Completing Tasks
Once you finish a certain number of items on your list, enjoy a calm break or snack. This approach can help you stay focused by pairing work with small pleasures.

Encouraging Positive Daily Mindset

A daily routine includes not just physical tasks, but also a mental outlook. How you speak to yourself in your mind can shape your entire day. Because Taurus is often practical and patient, building a positive mindset can further enhance the sense of peace:

Morning Affirmations
Right after waking up, you might take a moment to think a simple, kind statement, such as "I can handle my tasks today in a calm way."

Focus on Small Successes
If you got to work on time or completed a chore early, take a second to feel pleased about it. These small achievements can add up to a good mood.

Gentle Self-Correction
When something goes wrong, avoid harsh self-talk. Instead, you could say, "I made a mistake, but I can fix it by doing XYZ."

End-of-Day Reflections
Before bed, note one thing that went well or that you are thankful for. This does not have to be big. Maybe you had a tasty lunch or finished an email you had been delaying. Ending the day on a positive note can help you sleep better.

Limit Negative Input
While it is good to stay informed, watching too many upsetting news stories or engaging in negative chatter can drain your mood. Setting limits on those inputs can keep your outlook steadier.

Building Long-Term Habits One Step at a Time

Taurus is well-suited to gradual progress. Some people try to change their entire routine overnight, which is often overwhelming. Instead, Taurus can benefit from a slower approach:

Identify Key Areas for Change
Maybe you want to exercise more, improve your diet, or spend more time reading. Pick one area at a time rather than trying to fix everything.

Set Achievable Goals
For instance, if you want to read more, start with 10 minutes each evening. If you want more physical activity, try 10 minutes of walking daily. Over time, you can expand these goals.

Track Progress Simply
A small chart on the fridge or a basic app on your phone can remind you of daily steps. Taurus finds comfort in seeing a visual record of how they are doing.

Include Rewards
Each week or month, if you keep to your new habit, do something gentle that you enjoy. This can keep you motivated without needing anything flashy.

Adapt if Needed
If a new habit does not work well after a few weeks, adjust it. Taurus might resist changing the plan, but staying flexible can make a habit easier to maintain.

Social Routines and Community Involvement

Another aspect of daily life for Taurus is how they connect with others. While Taurus often enjoys smaller circles, having supportive social routines can add warmth to each day:

Regular Check-Ins
Planning a quick call or message to a close friend can become part of your routine. It helps maintain bonds without requiring large gatherings.

Shared Meals
If you live with family or a roommate, sharing at least one meal together daily (or a few times a week) can bring closeness. Taurus might enjoy cooking something basic but comforting, and the shared moment can deepen ties.

Local Groups or Clubs
If you have an interest—like gardening, crafts, or a gentle sport—checking out a local club can fill a small part of your weekly routine with socializing in a structured way. Taurus can find comfort in a predictable group schedule.

Digital Groups
If you prefer to stay at home or cannot travel, you could join an online community that matches an interest, like a forum for discussing cooking tips. Taurus might appreciate how these communities run on consistent posting and shared topics.

Respecting Alone Time
Even if you join a group, remember to keep some personal space. Taurus needs a balance between being around friends and having quiet moments to recharge.

Special Situations: Holidays or Busy Seasons

Life includes periods when routines are harder to keep—like festive times or busy work stretches. Taurus might feel uneasy if their normal schedule is disrupted. Here are some ideas to stay grounded:

Keep One or Two Core Habits
 Even if everything around you changes, try to keep a small piece of your routine intact—like a morning stretch or a nightly reading time. This anchor can help you feel stable.

Plan Break Times
 During busy periods, carve out a few minutes for rest, so you do not burn out. Even a short pause can help you reset.

Stay Flexible with Meal Times
 If the schedule is off, pack snacks or quick meals. Taurus values comfortable eating, so preparing in advance can prevent stress when you cannot follow your usual routine.

Communicate Your Needs
 If you are with friends or family who have a different pace, let them know if you need a calm moment. Taurus might do better in celebrations if they can slip away for a quiet walk or short rest.

Reflect Afterwards
 Once the busy time ends, see what went well and what could be done differently next time to keep you feeling balanced.

Handling Habit Overlaps and Conflicts

Sometimes, two habits might clash. For example, you want to go to bed early, but you also have a habit of scrolling through your phone at night. Taurus, with their steady approach, might find it tricky to switch quickly. Some suggestions:

Rank Your Priorities
Decide which habit is more important. If better sleep matters more, you might choose to turn off devices by a certain hour.

Replace, Do Not Just Remove
If you drop a habit like nighttime phone use, try replacing it with reading or listening to soft music. A direct swap can be easier for Taurus than simply cutting out a behavior.

Seek Moderation
Instead of never touching your phone at night, maybe limit it to 10 minutes. This middle route can keep your routine stable without feeling overly restricted.

Trial Period
Give yourself a set number of days or weeks to try a new arrangement. Knowing it is a test can help you feel less pressure.

Supportive Tools
If you need help, you can set phone alarms or use a reminder app. Taurus likes having clear prompts, so these tools can guide you gently.

CHAPTER 14: MYTHS ABOUT TAURUS

In astrology, each sign has gained certain stereotypes over time. People might say, "Taurus is always stubborn," or "Taurus only cares about money." Some of these ideas may contain bits of truth, but they often skip over the full picture of who Taurus really is. Myths or oversimplified views can lead people to misunderstand the sign, not seeing the complexity that lies beneath.

This chapter will discuss some common myths about Taurus, explain how they might have started, and offer a more rounded view. By clearing up these misconceptions, we can better appreciate the positive sides of Taurus and also see how each trait can have more than one angle. A Taurus person is not just one quality or behavior; like everyone, they have a wide range of feelings, interests, and abilities.

Myth: "Taurus Is Always Lazy"

One of the most repeated myths about Taurus is that they are lazy or dislike effort. Some believe this because Taurus is often seen as calm or slow-moving. It is true that a Taurus may not like rushing into things or running around with no plan. They also prize comfort and sometimes move at a measured pace. However, labeling them as lazy misses a lot of the real story.

Hard Work Behind the Scenes
 A Taurus can put in steady, consistent work for a long time. While they might not shout about their efforts, they keep going until they

reach their goal. Many Taurus individuals take pride in doing tasks properly, which can actually require a great deal of effort.

Slow but Productive
People might label them as "lazy" if they expect Taurus to move at lightning speed. But Taurus's slower rhythm often means they are thorough, paying attention to details. This method can lead to better, longer-lasting results.

Need for Rest
Everyone needs rest, and Taurus may be more open about valuing downtime. Instead of seeing that as laziness, think of it as balancing work with relaxation. A well-rested Taurus is often more productive in the long run.

So, while Taurus may appear leisurely at times, many of them are far from lazy. They simply prefer a calmer style of action and know how to pace themselves in a way that prevents burnout.

Myth: "Taurus Only Cares About Money and Possessions"

Another common misconception is that Taurus focuses solely on wealth, material items, or physical comforts. This myth might come from the fact that Taurus is associated with money in astrology and that many Taurus individuals like cozy surroundings. However, saying they "only" care about these things can be misleading.

Seeking Security, Not Just Luxury
While Taurus does appreciate comfortable items, the deeper motive is often security. Having a stable home, reliable income, and enough savings to handle emergencies helps a Taurus feel safe. It is not just about fancy things; it is about building a life that feels stable.

Practical Spending

Many Taurus people do not throw money away on showy items. Instead, they invest in quality goods that will last a long time. A Taurus might choose a well-made coat that can be worn for years, rather than multiple cheaper ones.

Generosity and Sharing

Taurus can be generous when they feel secure themselves. They might cook hearty meals for friends or buy gifts for loved ones. They value comfort but enjoy sharing it with those they care about.

It is true that money and physical comfort matter to many Taurus folks, yet that does not mean they lack depth or care nothing for emotional ties. They often see financial safety as a foundation that lets them support themselves and others.

Myth: "Taurus Cannot Handle Any Change"

Because Taurus prefers stability, there is a myth that they refuse all change. While it is true that big, fast changes can make Taurus uneasy, they are not stuck in stone. They simply want to feel sure about each step before moving forward.

Slower Adaptation

Taurus can adapt, but they usually prefer to do so at a measured pace. They might need time to understand the reason behind the shift and how it will affect them.

Selective Change

If the change seems practical and beneficial, a Taurus will eventually come around. They are not against making life better—they only resist sudden or illogical shifts that do not give them time to prepare.

Life Teaches Adaptability

Many Taurus individuals have experienced changes in jobs, relationships, or living situations. Over time, they learn to manage these events, even if they approach them with caution. This learning process can make Taurus quite capable of handling transitions, as long as they see the sense in them.

Thus, saying Taurus "cannot handle any change" is too narrow. They may be slower to jump on board, but they often do handle change once they see it is necessary or advantageous.

Myth: "Taurus Is Always Stubborn or Headstrong"

One of the biggest stereotypes about Taurus is their stubbornness. While it is true that Taurus can stand firm in their opinions, there is more to it than just being obstinate.

Steadfast vs. Stubborn

Taurus individuals can be steadfast, meaning once they commit to something, they will not easily quit. This trait can be a huge benefit in tasks that require persistence. Yet, it can become stubbornness if they ignore all new information.

Rooted in Values

Often, Taurus stands their ground because of strong personal values. For example, if they believe in fairness or loyalty, they may refuse to back down if they see something that goes against these beliefs.

Open to Reason

Taurus might not shift their view rapidly, but if someone calmly explains why a change or another viewpoint might be better, they can consider it. This is why discussing the facts or logic behind a plan can be more effective than pressuring them.

Yes, Taurus can be quite firm, but it is not always a negative trait. In many situations, their steadfastness helps them stick with tasks or stand up for what is right.

Myth: "Taurus Lacks Imagination or Creativity"

Because Taurus is an earth sign, some assume they only care about practical matters and lack creative sparks. While they do like things that are grounded, that does not mean they cannot be artistic or imaginative.

Love of Beauty
Taurus is often linked with Venus, the planet of love and beauty, suggesting they can have a strong sense of aesthetics. Many Taurus individuals show creativity in cooking, decorating, painting, music, or fashion. They want their environment to look and feel pleasing, which can lead to artful expression.

Hands-On Creativity
Taurus might be more inclined to practical arts, like pottery, gardening, or making crafts that you can use daily. Their creative side often links to tangible outcomes, blending imagination with a useful end product.

Steady Artistic Progress
Instead of wild bursts of inspiration, Taurus might develop their creative projects over time. They might keep refining a painting, a knitting project, or a garden plan until it achieves a pleasing result.

So, saying Taurus lacks creativity is a myth. They just channel it in ways that often have a physical or real-world component. Their creativity can be subtle but quite significant.

Myth: "Taurus Only Eats and Sleeps"

Sometimes, people poke fun at Taurus by suggesting all they do is lounge, eat, and sleep. While Taurus does value rest and good meals, they are not limited to these pursuits.

Balanced Approach to Leisure
Taurus does appreciate comfortable rest and enjoys tasty treats, but that is only one part of life. They work steadily, handle responsibilities, and often have various hobbies.

Hobby and Career Focus
Many Taurus individuals take pride in their work or personal interests, devoting consistent energy to them. They may invest time learning new skills or advancing in a job, proving they are far from lazy or uninterested in growth.

Healthier Choices
While a Taurus may enjoy hearty meals, many also look for balanced diets over time. They might relish cooking or baking, choosing fresh ingredients. Rest is important to them, but they know the value of activity as well.

Yes, Taurus likes comfort, but it is unfair to say they only focus on food and sleep. They can be quite dedicated to their duties and their personal development, balancing rest with necessary action.

Myth: "Taurus Is Always Calm and Never Gets Upset"

Taurus has a reputation for being laid-back, but that does not mean they do not experience strong emotions. They can be patient, but like everyone, they have limits.

Slow-Burning Emotions
Rather than reacting immediately, Taurus might keep their feelings

inside until a certain point. If pushed too far, they can have a strong reaction.

Protective Anger
Taurus can become upset if they or someone they care about is threatened. Their loyal nature means they will defend what they hold dear.

Preference for Harmony
They try to keep situations calm, so they do not show anger as readily as some other signs might. However, beneath that calm exterior, they can still feel tension or frustration.

While Taurus can seem cool and collected most of the time, suggesting they "never get upset" ignores the reality that they can feel deeply. They just express it differently or take longer to reach a boiling point.

Myth: "Taurus Has No Interest in Personal Growth"

Some might think Taurus is so fixed in their ways that they do not care about improving or learning. This myth can appear because Taurus is known for routine and comfort.

Steady Self-Improvement
Taurus often approaches personal growth with the same methodical style they use for everything else. They might learn new skills or refine existing ones slowly and steadily.

Willingness to Learn in Their Own Time
Taurus prefers to see real value before they commit to a growth path. If they see that learning a new skill or making a lifestyle change will truly help them, they are usually willing to do the work.

Life Lessons

Over time, life experiences teach them that adaptability can be necessary. This can lead to genuine personal changes, but they might not trumpet these changes loudly. Instead, they apply them quietly.

Taurus does value stability, but that does not mean they stand still forever. Many put in long-term effort to become better in areas that matter to them.

Myth: "Taurus Is Not Emotional or Caring"

Sometimes, because Taurus is not as openly dramatic as some signs, people think they do not care about feelings. This could not be further from the truth.

Steady Care

Taurus shows love through consistent support, small acts of service, and loyalty. They might not be the loudest about their affection, but they often show it in tangible ways.

Listening Ear

A Taurus friend can be a patient listener. They may offer thoughtful advice based on real-life practicality. This can be very comforting to someone in need.

Private Emotions

Taurus tends to keep deeper feelings tucked away until they trust the other person. So, they do have emotions; they just do not let everyone see them right away.

In reality, Taurus can be quite caring, yet they express it more quietly. They might cook a meal for a sick friend, help someone with a chore, or provide dependable companionship over many years.

Myth: "Taurus Does Not Like to Socialize"

Another myth is that Taurus always prefers to be alone. While they do enjoy calm and personal space, Taurus can also value friendships, family, and group activities—just in a more measured way.

Quality Over Quantity
Taurus might have fewer but closer friends. They enjoy smaller gatherings where they can have real conversations, rather than big noisy parties.

Stable Bonds
Once a Taurus invests in a friendship, they usually keep it going for a long time. They are not typically social butterflies, but they do appreciate meaningful connections.

Comfortable Social Events
Taurus might like gatherings that center on good food, casual games, or relaxed settings. They might not race around making new acquaintances, but they can be quite warm with people they know.

So, Taurus is not necessarily a loner. They just have a specific style of socializing that focuses on true bonds, comfort, and deeper discussions.

Myth: "Taurus Never Takes Risks"

Being cautious by nature does not equate to being unwilling to take any risks. Taurus might weigh options carefully, but that does not mean they avoid every challenge.

Calculated Risks
Taurus will likely do research before taking a leap. They might see if an idea has a high chance of success. If it does, they can be surprisingly determined to follow through.

Practical Priorities
They might invest in property, start a small business, or switch careers if they see a logical path that can lead to stability. Although these moves contain risk, Taurus feels better if they can plan steps clearly.

Steadfast Pursuit
When a Taurus does decide to take a risk, they usually follow through with consistent effort. It might not be flashy, but they put in the hard work behind the scenes.

Hence, it is not correct to claim Taurus never tries anything risky. They simply like to know what they are stepping into and keep a realistic plan to guide them.

Myth: "All Taurus People Act Exactly the Same"

A big myth is that everyone born under Taurus is identical. Astrology can be fun, but individuals are shaped by many factors beyond a single sun sign.

Unique Charts
Besides the sun sign, each person has a moon sign, rising sign, and other planet positions. These can alter how Taurus energy appears in someone's personality.

Personal Experiences
Life events, upbringing, culture, and personal choices matter just as much—if not more—than zodiac signs. A Taurus raised in a bustling city might develop different habits than one raised in a rural area.

Individual Traits
Even two Taurus individuals with similar birth charts can differ in how they handle daily life, relationships, and challenges. One might be more outwardly friendly, while the other is more reserved.

So, while certain broad qualities often show up in Taurus, it is oversimplified to imagine they all behave exactly the same. Each person is unique, shaped by a mix of factors.

Where These Myths May Come From

How did these false ideas become so widespread? A few likely reasons:

Simplicity in Horoscopes
Many short horoscopes in newspapers or online try to summarize each sign with just a few traits. This can lead to oversimplified views—like "Taurus = stubborn and materialistic."

Stories and Cultural References
Films, books, or jokes might portray a stereotypical Taurus character who overindulges in food or naps all day. Repetition of these images can stick in people's minds.

Misreading Calm Behavior
Taurus's steady and patient approach can be interpreted as laziness or lack of creativity if someone expects quick, flashy responses.

Partial Truth
Some myths contain a small grain of truth. For instance, Taurus does like comfort. But exaggerating it to "they only eat and sleep" ignores all the other aspects of their personality.

Why Busting Myths Matters

It is easy to make quick judgments about others based on broad labels. Yet, seeing beyond myths can improve how people get along, whether at work, in friendships, or in families. Taurus can feel misunderstood if people assume these stereotypes. Meanwhile, others might miss out on the true strengths a Taurus offers, such as loyalty, steady effort, and practical thinking.

By recognizing that a Taurus is more than just a single trait, we open the door to real understanding. This can lead to better communication, deeper trust, and a fair chance for each person to be seen in their full light.

Embracing the Real Taurus

How can we move past myths and appreciate the real Taurus qualities?

Ask Them
Instead of assuming, talk to a Taurus friend or family member about their preferences, goals, and hopes. First-hand conversation is often better than stereotypes.

Notice Their Effort
Take note if they are working quietly behind the scenes or staying true to their word over a long period. These consistent acts might not be flashy, but they matter.

Encourage Their Strengths
If you see a Taurus has a talent for thoughtful planning or creativity with hands-on tasks, support them. This can help them shine.

Respect Their Pace
When suggesting something new, give them enough information and a bit of time to think it over. This respects their process and might lead to a smoother result.

Recognize Complexities
A Taurus might love good meals and nice fabrics, but they can also

care about relationships, personal growth, and new experiences, as long as they feel safe enough to explore them.

Reminders for Taurus Dealing with Stereotypes

If you are a Taurus who feels judged by these myths, here are a few thoughts:

Stay True to Yourself
You do not have to prove anything to people who hold narrow views. Keep working at your own steady pace and let results speak for themselves.

Communicate Kindly
If loved ones or coworkers treat you like you are stubborn or lazy, consider calmly explaining your reasoning. They may not realize how thorough your thought process is.

Embrace the Positive Aspects
Being patient, steady, and comfort-loving can be strengths. Share with others how these qualities benefit your life and your relationships.

Avoid Overreacting
Getting angry at stereotypes might reinforce the idea of Taurus as stubborn or easily annoyed. A calm approach often shows your true nature more effectively.

Over time, people who see your real behavior will understand that you are not just a label, but a multi-layered individual with a lot to offer.

Other Astrological Factors That Affect Taurus Traits

Since we have mentioned that not all Taurus people are identical, it can help to know some additional factors in astrology:

Moon Sign
Influences your emotional style. A Taurus sun with a moon in Aries might be quicker to speak out, while a Taurus sun with a moon in Cancer might be very gentle and caring.

Rising Sign (Ascendant)
Affects how you present yourself to the world. A Taurus with a Leo rising may seem more outgoing, while a Taurus with a Pisces rising might appear more dreamy.

Other Planet Placements
Mercury, Venus, Mars, and so forth can color your thinking, romance, and energy. These placements can create big differences among Taurus individuals.

Transits and Progressions
Current planetary movements can also influence your daily mood and behavior. You might have a phase where you are more open to change than usual.

Knowing these aspects reveals how each Taurus can vary greatly, helping us see why the myths do not apply to everyone in the same way.

Learning from Taurus Traits

People from all signs can learn from the real essence of Taurus:

Patience and Persistence
Taurus teaches us to keep going step by step. Rather than giving up when challenges appear, we can steadily work through them.

Loyalty and Reliability
Being the friend or colleague who shows up on time and sticks around can create a strong foundation in any group.

Appreciation of Comfort and Beauty
Making your space pleasant and taking time to enjoy small luxuries can enrich daily life without turning you into someone only focused on things.

Sense of Security
While it is not healthy to chase security too intensely, having a basic safety net—like a small savings or stable routines—can reduce anxiety.

These qualities can benefit anyone, not just those born under Taurus.

Correcting a Myth in Real Life

If you encounter someone who repeats a myth—like "Taurus never tries new things"—how can you respond?

Share an Example
You might point out a Taurus friend who took up a novel hobby or changed careers successfully. Real-life stories often break stereotypes.

Mention the Bigger Picture
Explain that Taurus might be cautious, but they do change once they see the logic or plan. This highlights the difference between caution and outright refusal.

Stay Polite

Arguing aggressively can feed the stubbornness myth. Instead, speak calmly about what you have learned.

By handling these moments kindly, you can help spread more accurate views and possibly open others' eyes to the richness of the Taurus character.

CHAPTER 15: TAURUS AND PASTIMES

A pastime is an activity that people do in their free time for enjoyment or relaxation. Different signs in astrology might be linked with certain pastimes that appeal to their usual styles, but each person is unique, and individual preferences vary. Still, many Taurus individuals share common traits, such as valuing calm, comfort, and steady progress. These traits can shape the kinds of hobbies and free-time activities they are likely to find fulfilling.

In this chapter, we will look at the range of pastimes Taurus often enjoys, including artistic, physical, and social activities. We will discuss how Taurus might approach these interests and why they can be beneficial. We will also explore how Taurus can keep a sense of balance, making sure their leisure time remains satisfying without leading to boredom. By the end, you should have a clearer idea of how a Taurus can get the most out of pastimes that match their natural style.

Why Pastimes Matter for Taurus

A pastime is not only a way to pass the time—it can bring relaxation, reduce stress, and provide personal growth. For Taurus, who likes stability and calm, having regular, comforting pastimes can do wonders for their mood and overall health. Here are a few reasons why choosing the right hobbies can be important for a Taurus:

Relaxation and Stress Relief
Taurus often values a sense of peace. After dealing with day-to-day tasks, a good pastime can let them unwind and recover.

Personal Satisfaction

When a Taurus sees steady improvement or creates something tangible, they can gain a sense of achievement. This matches their methodical approach to life.

Routine and Comfort

Working a pastime into daily or weekly routines can help Taurus maintain a steady rhythm. Activities that give them joy can become reliable highlights they look forward to.

Social or Solo Engagement

Taurus can pick whether they prefer group-based hobbies that let them bond with others or solo activities that provide peaceful, individual focus. Both can be meaningful.

By focusing on hobbies that fit their nature, Taurus can nourish both mind and body, ensuring that free time is not just empty but truly rewarding.

Artistic and Creative Pastimes

One misconception, as we have discussed, is that Taurus lacks imagination. In fact, many Taurus individuals have a strong creative side, especially in fields that involve the senses or tangible results. Here are some artistic hobbies that often appeal to Taurus:

Painting and Drawing

Creating visual art can allow Taurus to work slowly, focusing on detail and texture. They might prefer mediums like oil or watercolor, which suit a careful, layered approach.

Pottery and Sculpting

Using clay and feeling the material with their hands can be quite grounding for Taurus. They can form shapes at their own pace, enjoying the tactile connection to the earth.

Music Appreciation or Performance

While not all Taurus individuals will perform music, many like soothing tunes or melodic soundscapes. Some might learn an instrument slowly over time, building confidence with each practice session.

Crafts and DIY Projects

Sewing, knitting, woodworking, or other crafts can suit Taurus perfectly. These tasks let them see concrete progress and produce something useful, whether it is a scarf, a shelf, or a handmade card.

A key reason these arts may appeal is because Taurus enjoys activities with tangible outcomes. Being able to look at a finished piece of pottery or hear themselves play a song can bring a real sense of completion and pride.

Culinary and Home-Related Pastimes

Taurus is often linked to comfort, which can include an appreciation for good food and a welcoming home environment. It is no surprise that many Taurus folks find joy in pastimes that involve cooking or caring for their living space.

Cooking and Baking

Because taste is an important sense, Taurus can take pleasure in making new dishes. Trying a fresh recipe or perfecting a family favorite can give them a chance to use their careful nature. They might experiment with different flavors, but once they find a recipe that works, they may keep refining it until it is just right.

Gardening

This can be a strong match for an earth sign. Seeing plants grow day by day, watering them, and watching them flower or bear fruit can satisfy Taurus's steady approach. Whether it is a few pots on a balcony or a larger garden, nurturing green life can be grounding.

Interior Decorating
 Taurus likes comfortable surroundings, so rearranging furniture, choosing calming colors for walls, or adding decorative touches can be fun. They might not make big changes often, but small updates—like new cushions or a different layout—can refresh the home.

Collecting Kitchen Tools
 Some Taurus individuals enjoy finding the best utensils or cookware. They may spend time reading about which kitchen gadget is most durable or efficient, seeing it as a small hobby that improves daily life.

These home-centered activities let Taurus bring comfort right to their living space. The calm focus they use in cooking or gardening can become a soothing routine that helps them forget the stresses of the outside world.

Physical and Outdoor Activities

Some people associate Taurus with restfulness, yet many Taurus individuals like moderate physical activities that let them move at a measured pace. These can offer health benefits and help them stay connected to nature or their bodies without feeling rushed or overwhelmed.

Walking or Hiking
 A simple walk in a park or a light hike can provide just enough movement. Taurus can pause to enjoy the scenery, rather than racing up the trail. If they have a dog or a friend who wants to tag along, even better.

Biking at Leisure
 Competitive cycling might not be the usual Taurus choice, but a slow, scenic bike ride can match their preference for calm

exploration. Having a comfortable, reliable bike is usually important to them.

Yoga or Stretching
Activities that blend gentle movement with relaxation are often a good fit. Yoga or simple daily stretches can reduce tension and align with Taurus's steady approach.

Gardening (Again, But Outdoors)
We mentioned gardening under home-related pastimes, but it is also a physical activity that involves bending, digging, and carrying tools. Taurus can enjoy mild exercise while being close to the earth.

These moderate exercises help Taurus stay healthy and grounded without forcing them into overly fast or competitive sports. They can go step by step, focusing on their own comfort level and progress.

Social Pastimes and Group Settings

While Taurus can be happy in solitude, some also enjoy pastimes that involve friends or community. This does not mean huge crowds or noisy events, but rather smaller, comfortable gatherings.

Cooking Groups or Potluck Dinners
A Taurus might join a group of friends to try out new recipes together, or host a cozy dinner where everyone contributes a dish. This blends their love for food with a friendly atmosphere.

Book Clubs
If they enjoy reading, a Taurus might appreciate a low-stress book club. They can take their time reading and then discuss thoughts in a calm, relaxed setting.

Crafting Circles
Groups that meet to knit, sew, or do other crafts can be comforting for Taurus. They can work on their personal project while chatting with like-minded people.

Board Game Nights
Some Taurus folks find board games appealing, especially if the pace is not too frantic. Strategy games let them think carefully, while simpler party games can be fun if the atmosphere stays friendly rather than competitive.

In these social pastimes, Taurus can enjoy connection without feeling rushed or bombarded by constant change. They can take comfort in a stable routine: the same group members, a regular meeting time, and familiar, pleasant surroundings.

Travel as a Pastime, Done Taurus-Style

Not all Taurus individuals travel often, since they value home comforts. But for those who do enjoy seeing new places, they might prefer a style of travel that balances exploration with relaxation. Here are some ways a Taurus may approach going somewhere:

Well-Planned Trips
Taurus might carefully choose a location with good accommodations, pleasant scenery, or known activities that fit their slower pace. Rushed tours might feel stressful, so they usually pick places where they can settle in.

Enjoying Local Foods
Food is a big draw. Taurus might research local cuisine in advance and look forward to trying dishes that are fresh or famous in that region.

Comfortable Lodgings
They might spend extra money to ensure a nice room with a cozy bed. Even on a budget trip, they often prioritize a clean, comfortable environment over being extremely thrifty.

Mix of Rest and Light Adventures
Taurus may take short outings to see nature or local attractions, then return to a comfortable spot to rest. They do not need to check off every landmark to feel fulfilled.

This approach to seeing new places suits the Taurus preference for comfort and measured experiences, rather than hectic schedules and sudden changes.

Balancing Hobbies and Responsibilities

While pastimes can enrich life, Taurus also takes duties seriously—whether that is work, family needs, or financial security. Sometimes, a Taurus might worry that too much free-time fun conflicts with their responsibilities. To maintain harmony:

Set Time Blocks
Taurus can schedule a fixed time for a hobby so it does not interfere with other tasks. For example, one hour of painting after dinner, or a gardening session on Saturday mornings.

Combine Social and Hobbies
If they have limited time, a Taurus could merge friend meet-ups with their hobby. For instance, invite a friend over to help with a simple cooking project. This way, they get both social time and a pastime in one go.

Use Hobbies as Stress Relief
When stressed by deadlines or responsibilities, a short break to

engage in a relaxing pastime might actually boost energy and focus. Taurus often comes back to tasks calmer and more productive.

Review Priorities
If the pastime begins to dominate too much time—perhaps they are shopping for new cooking tools every day instead of focusing on bills—they can step back and re-balance. Taurus usually does well setting practical limits.

By keeping these guidelines in mind, Taurus can enjoy their leisure activities without feeling they are neglecting other parts of life.

Trying New Interests

While Taurus likes the familiar, it can be healthy to occasionally pick up a fresh activity. This helps prevent getting bored or stuck in a rut. Some strategies for expanding hobbies:

Tiny Steps
Taurus can start small. If they want to try painting but have never touched a brush, they could buy basic supplies and practice a few minutes a day. Over time, they gain confidence.

Look for Classes or Groups
If they feel unsure, a gentle class or workshop might help them learn in a structured environment. Taurus can see how they like it before fully committing.

Pair with a Friend
Sometimes going into something new with a buddy can reduce anxiety. Having support may lessen the reluctance to try.

Allow Trial Period
Taurus can set a time, say two months, to see if they enjoy the new

pastime. If it is not a good fit, they can walk away without guilt. But if they do enjoy it, they have found a new avenue of relaxation.

Being open to fresh pastimes—while still keeping the main comforts of daily routine—can spark new excitement in a Taurus's life.

Avoiding Overindulgence

Because Taurus likes comfort and can develop strong attachments to certain enjoyments, there is a risk of overindulging. This might be overspending on collectibles, over-snacking, or spending too many hours on a screen-based hobby.

Set Reasonable Limits
 If a Taurus loves collecting rare items, they can decide on a monthly budget. If they like cooking sweet treats, they can limit themselves to a moderate portion rather than overdoing it.

Balance with Healthy Choices
 For each indulgent pastime—like watching TV for hours—try to add a more active or socially engaging one. This way, they are not just sitting too much.

Ask Trusted Friends for Input
 If a Taurus is unsure whether they are overdoing an activity, they can check with a close friend or family member. Outside perspectives can help them notice if a hobby is taking up too much time or money.

Use Self-Reflection
 Taurus might reflect on why they turn to a certain hobby. If it is purely for calm and fun, that is fine, but if it is avoiding real-life problems, it may be time to address those problems directly.

Striking the right balance between enjoyment and moderation ensures that Taurus's activities stay beneficial rather than becoming habits that cause harm or block progress.

Pastimes for Mental Stimulation

Though Taurus often enjoys crafts, cooking, or nature walks, they can also benefit from hobbies that keep the mind sharp. A few mentally stimulating pastimes might include:

Puzzles and Strategy Games
 Crosswords, Sudoku, jigsaw puzzles, or strategy board games can suit a Taurus's methodical thinking style. They enjoy taking their time, sorting pieces, and seeing the final result.

Reading Nonfiction
 Taurus might be drawn to practical books—like guides about home improvement, gardening, or personal finance. Reading these can boost knowledge in areas that match their daily life.

Writing or Journaling
 Some Taurus individuals find calm in expressing their thoughts on paper. They might keep a journal where they list observations, daily reflections, or ideas for the future.

Online Learning
 If they are comfortable with technology, Taurus might sign up for an online class in a skill they find interesting, such as photography or basic accounting. They will move at a measured pace, reviewing videos as needed.

These mental hobbies can help Taurus stay engaged while also adding new tools or insights to their life.

Seasonal Pastimes

Because Taurus is an earth sign linked to the flow of nature, certain hobbies might feel more appealing in specific seasons.

Spring
Many Taurus individuals enjoy spring gardening, watching new growth, or going on walks to see blooming flowers. They might also do spring cleaning, refreshing their home environment after winter.

Summer
Light outdoor activities—like picnics, mild hikes, or short beach trips—allow them to enjoy good weather without extreme sports. Cooking fresh produce from a local market can also be a summer treat.

Autumn
Harvest season can be special if they have a garden or attend a local farm event. Some might like collecting colorful leaves or making warm, cozy meals like soups and stews.

Winter
Indoors, activities such as baking bread, knitting, or crocheting might become more frequent. A Taurus could also host small gatherings where everyone shares hot drinks and conversation.

Linking hobbies to the changing seasons can keep Taurus from feeling stuck in a single pattern all year round. They can adjust activities to match the natural cycle of the environment.

Pastimes for Introverted or Extroverted Taurus

Not all Taurus individuals have the same social preferences, so the choice of hobbies can differ:

Introverted Taurus
They might prefer quiet, solo activities like reading, painting, or writing. They could still meet with a small group of close friends once in a while.

Extroverted Taurus
Some Taurus folks enjoy a bit more social buzz—though typically not extremely loud environments. They might host small cooking parties, go on mild group outings, or do craft sessions with friends.

Hybrid Approach
Many Taurus people fall somewhere in between. They might alternate between alone time and small social gatherings, choosing hobbies that let them do both comfortably.

Understanding one's own level of comfort with social interaction helps Taurus pick suitable pastimes that do not leave them feeling drained.

Using Pastimes as Self-Care

We touched on self-care for Taurus in another chapter, but it is worth highlighting how hobbies can also support mental and emotional wellness:

Mindful Engagement
When a Taurus is knitting or painting, they can focus on the task at hand, putting aside worries about the past or future. This mindful state can calm the mind.

Release and Expression
Creative hobbies can give an outlet for emotions. If they feel stressed or upset, shaping clay or writing a short poem might help them process feelings quietly.

Grounding Through the Senses
Activities like cooking or gardening stimulate smell, touch, and taste. Focusing on these senses can bring Taurus into the present moment, reducing anxiety.

Boosting Confidence
Finishing a project or learning a new skill can remind Taurus that they are capable and steady, which can be reassuring during tough times.

In this way, pastimes serve more than just entertainment—they can be an essential part of nurturing a Taurus's well-being.

Finding Community Through Hobbies

When a pastime aligns with a group, it can create a sense of belonging. For Taurus, who values trust and closeness, building friendships through shared interests can be especially rewarding:

Local Clubs or Workshops
Joining a local gardening club, craft workshop, or cooking group can help Taurus expand social ties while doing something they enjoy.

Online Communities
If local options are limited, online communities or forums dedicated to a hobby can also offer support, advice, and camaraderie, all at Taurus's chosen pace.

Hosting or Sharing
A Taurus who feels comfortable might host a small meet-up or event at home, inviting people who share the same pastime. This merges the Taurus love of home comfort with social bonding.

Long-Term Friendships
Because Taurus is loyal, they often build lasting friendships with

people they see regularly in a hobby group. Over time, these connections can become a strong support network.

This sense of community can deepen a pastime, making it more meaningful and providing social benefits as well.

Pastimes and Lifelong Learning

Taurus often likes the idea of building skills slowly over time. Certain hobbies can grow with them for years or even decades, matching their patient nature:

Music Instrument Mastery
 Learning guitar, piano, or violin can span a lifetime. Taurus can practice a bit each day, enjoying gradual improvements in skill and confidence.

Gardening Expansion
 Starting with a few houseplants can evolve into a larger garden as Taurus becomes more comfortable. Each season can bring new lessons about soil, watering, and plant care.

Cooking Adventures
 Cooking can start with basics and progress to gourmet dishes. Over years, a Taurus home cook might develop a personal style or even share recipes with friends and family.

Handcrafting Expertise
 Knitting, sewing, or woodworking can shift from a simple pastime to a more advanced craft. They might make gifts for loved ones or even sell items for extra income if they wish.

This long-term approach fits Taurus's inclination to develop mastery. Instead of rushing, they can gradually expand their knowledge, building strong abilities and deeper satisfaction.

Dealing with Boredom or Ruts in Hobbies

Even with a favorite pastime, a Taurus might occasionally feel stuck or bored. Because they like familiarity, they might not notice right away that they are in a rut. Here are ways to refresh:

Add a Small Twist
If a Taurus loves cooking Italian dishes, maybe they can try a recipe from another country that still feels somewhat similar. This small shift can spark renewed interest.

Involve Another Person
Inviting a friend who has new insights can change the dynamic. They might suggest a technique or perspective that the Taurus never considered.

Change the Setting
If they always paint in the same corner of the house, maybe try painting in the yard or near a window with different light. A new environment can stir fresh ideas.

Take a Short Break
If the hobby feels stale, stepping away for a little while might rekindle the spark. Taurus can focus on another activity, then return later with new enthusiasm.

By recognizing the signs of boredom, a Taurus can adjust in a gentle way, staying open to minor changes that keep the pastime fulfilling.

Encouraging Children or Younger Relatives Who Are Taurus

If you have a child, sibling, or younger relative who shows Taurus traits, helping them find suitable pastimes can guide them toward healthy growth. Some approaches:

Offer Options
Present a variety of hands-on or creative hobbies—like simple crafts, cooking, or gardening—and let them pick what interests them.

Avoid High Pressure
Taurus might freeze up if forced into an activity with strict deadlines or intense competition. Provide gentle guidance and let them explore at a comfortable pace.

Praise Steady Progress
Acknowledge small improvements, like learning a few new chords on an instrument or growing a healthy plant from a seed. This encouragement rewards their patient nature.

Set Realistic Goals
If they pick a big project, break it into smaller steps so they do not feel overwhelmed. For instance, if they want to learn piano, focus on a few notes or a short song first.

By nurturing these qualities early, younger Taurus individuals can carry positive hobbies and self-confidence into adulthood.

Hobbies That Generate Extra Income

For Taurus who appreciate financial security, some pastimes might lead to small earnings if they choose to share or sell their creations:

Selling Crafts Online
Platforms for handmade items allow a Taurus to share knitted scarves, pottery, or jewelry they produce during free time.

Baking or Catering
If they love cooking, a Taurus might offer baked goods or small

catering services for local events. This can start with friends and family.

Home-Grown Produce
A Taurus with a decent garden might sell herbs, flowers, or vegetables at a local market. Even a small stall can bring a bit of extra income.

Tutoring or Teaching
If they become skilled at a hobby, they can give beginner lessons. For example, teaching basic guitar chords or showing someone how to start a mini herb garden.

This blend of pastime and practical gain can appeal to Taurus's desire for both comfort and stability, though it is important they keep it enjoyable and not let it become a stressful second job.

Avoiding a Pile of Unfinished Projects

Sometimes, Taurus can accumulate multiple hobbies or half-completed items. They start with enthusiasm but might lose interest if something becomes too challenging or if a new activity seems more appealing.

Prioritize
List out current hobbies and projects. Decide which ones you truly wish to finish and which can be put aside.

Set Small Completion Steps
If you have a half-finished piece of art, plan to do just 15 minutes on it each day. Breaking it down helps you push through.

Recycle or Repurpose
If there is a project you no longer like, see if you can transform it

into something else or reuse the materials. This way, you reduce waste and keep your environment tidy.

Learn from Past Abandoned Hobbies

Reflect on why you lost interest. Was it too complex? Did you lack guidance? Understanding the reason can help you pick future hobbies more wisely.

Keeping unfinished projects to a minimum can reduce clutter in both your home and mind, preserving the calm environment Taurus desires.

CHAPTER 16: TAURUS IN DIFFERENT CULTURES

The concept of Taurus is deeply tied to the zodiac as practiced in Western astrology, where it is the second sign linked to the Bull. But ideas resembling Taurus appear in other cultures' star lore or traditions, sometimes taking on different names and stories. Across various regions and historical periods, the bull or bull-like figures have been symbols of strength, fertility, or stability. This chapter will explore how the imagery and traits of Taurus or the bull show up in different cultural contexts around the world, and how these versions may or may not resemble the Western astrology Taurus we know today.

By looking at Taurus-like figures across ancient civilizations and modern cultural interpretations, we see shared themes: the idea of a steady power, a connection to the earth, and the importance of patience or loyalty. While each culture has its unique perspective, these parallels can be fascinating, showing how the bull symbol or a similar concept resonates with human life in many places.

The Bull in Ancient Civilizations

In ancient times, the bull was often a symbol of might, stability, and sometimes fertility. Many early civilizations respected the bull for its role in farming and its sheer physical power:

Mesopotamia
In some Mesopotamian myths, bulls appeared in tales of creation or were linked to gods of storm and agriculture. The bull's strength was seen as a sign of divine favor for growing crops.

Ancient Egypt
The Apis bull was honored in Memphis, representing strength and fertile land along the Nile. Egyptians saw the bull as a channel to certain gods and believed it carried holy power.

Indus Valley
Seals found from the Indus Valley Civilization often depict bulls, though it is not entirely clear what they symbolized. Scholars suggest it could relate to wealth, fertility, or revered resources in that region.

Early Greece and Crete
The Minoan culture on Crete famously had bull-leaping rituals. Bulls appeared in myths and art, perhaps symbolizing both nature's force and the cycle of life.

These early references do not exactly match modern astrology's Taurus, but they lay a foundation for associating the bull with stability, power, and the cycle of growth.

Taurus in Ancient Greek and Roman Astrology

Our modern zodiac system largely flows from ancient Greek and Roman traditions. The constellation of Taurus was recognized as a bull in Greek mythology, and stories about it often related to Zeus and transformations:

Myth of Europa
One famous tale says that Zeus, king of the gods, took the form of a white bull to carry the princess Europa across the sea. While not identical to how we see Taurus in personal traits, the story ties the bull shape in the sky to love, seduction, and power.

Roman Adaptations
The Romans continued much of the Greek astrological system but

gave gods Latin names. Taurus remained a bull in the Roman zodiac, symbolizing a robust and steadfast energy.

Link to Spring

In these systems, Taurus was associated with the season of spring, a period of growth and renewal. This matched the bull's symbolism of fertility and the earth's bounty.

While these classical stories do not mention daily behaviors of a Taurus person, they cemented the bull as a zodiac figure representing fertility, grounded energy, and a stable approach to life.

Near Eastern Influences

Zodiac concepts also spread through the Near East, where different cultures added local flavor:

Babylonian Astronomy

The Babylonians had a star map that included a "Bull of Heaven," which might have helped shape Greek ideas. Their detailed star catalogs were among the earliest.

Persian Traditions

Ancient Persia had influences from Babylonian star lore, and though the modern zodiac eventually took root in Persia, local myths sometimes blended with older narratives.

Hebrew References

While not strictly astrological, the biblical Golden Calf story shows how the bull or calf was seen as a potent symbol of wealth, worship, and sometimes misplaced devotion. It reflects the bull's strong cultural significance, though not in the same sense as a personal zodiac sign.

These influences show how the bull or Taurus-like figure traveled through trade routes, conquests, and cultural exchange, absorbing varied meanings along the way.

Taurus Symbolism in East Asian Thought

East Asian cultures had different systems of astrology, some overlapping with Western ideas and others distinct. The bull (or ox) appears in several forms:

Chinese Zodiac
The Chinese zodiac includes the Ox, not the Bull, though they are similar animals. The Ox is the second animal in the 12-year cycle. Like Taurus, the Ox is often said to be diligent, patient, and reliable, valuing routine and calm work. But this link is more about the nature of the Ox in Chinese tradition, not tied to monthly birth periods as in Western astrology.

Japan
Japan uses the same 12-year cycle from Chinese tradition, so a person born in the Year of the Ox might share those traits. However, Japan also historically borrowed from Chinese ideas while merging them with Shinto beliefs.

Korea
Similarly, Korea has the same 12-year cycle, calling it the Year of the Ox. People with that sign might be described in ways that loosely overlap with Taurus traits—steady, hardworking, and humble.

Differences from Western Taurus
While Western Taurus is an April–May sun sign, the East Asian Ox year covers an entire year determined by the lunar calendar, not a single month. Yet, the Ox's qualities can mirror certain Taurus qualities: patience, a strong work ethic, and a preference for consistent routines.

Thus, though the cultural context differs, one can find a sort of parallel in the respect for a steadfast, grounded nature associated with bull-like creatures.

Influence of the Bull in South Asian Traditions

South Asia, including India, has deep roots in astrology, though it often uses the sidereal zodiac rather than the tropical zodiac used in mainstream Western astrology. The bull is also meaningful in some local traditions:

Vedic Astrology
Called Jyotish, it has signs similar to Western ones but calculated by different methods. The sign comparable to Taurus is Vrishabha, which means "bull." People with a Vrishabha sun (or ascending sign) may be described in ways that align with what Western astrology calls Taurus: stable, patient, and focused on comfort.

Bull in Hindu Mythology
The bull Nandi is the vehicle of the god Shiva. Nandi is often seen outside Shiva temples, symbolizing devotion and strength. While not exactly a zodiac sign, it again underscores the bull's significance as a loyal figure that stands for faithfulness and calm power.

Cultural Celebrations
Various festivals in India might honor cattle for their role in agriculture. The bull's image as a gentle but strong provider can mirror some Taurus qualities, though this is not strictly an astrological link.

Thus, in South Asia, the bull also holds a notable place, sometimes blending spiritual devotion with the theme of reliability and grounded energy.

Taurus-Like Figures in the Celtic World

Celtic mythology, spanning areas like Ireland, Scotland, and Wales, had reverence for nature and animals:

Bull Symbols
Though the Celts did not have the same zodiac system, bulls appeared in their stories and artwork, representing courage, fertility, and sometimes a protector role.

The Táin Bó Cúailnge
Also called "The Cattle Raid of Cooley," this epic from Irish legend involves prized bulls, highlighting how important cattle were to Celtic wealth and status. While not about a single zodiac sign, it still shows a cultural respect for strong, valuable animals.

Seasonal Festivals
Some Celtic traditions revolve around the natural wheel of the year. The bull's role might be tied to the harvest or pastoral life, again linking it to ideas of stability and sustenance.

Although these references do not directly mention "Taurus" the zodiac sign, they reveal how Celtic culture also saw the bull as vital and strong, resonating with the broad Taurus themes of abundance, earthiness, and continuity.

The Bull in Nordic and Germanic Myths

Northern Europe had fewer direct references to the bull as a zodiac figure, yet there are glimpses of bull or ox images:

Germanic Tribes
They valued cattle as sources of wealth and symbols of property. While not specifically a bull cult, the significance of livestock in the economy was high.

Norse Mythology
Some references mention a primeval cow named Auðumbla, crucial in creation myths. Though not a bull, this being still stands for fertility and life-giving properties.

Regional Folklore
In parts of Scandinavia, local legends mention powerful or magical cattle, underscoring their role in survival. These stories might remind us of Taurus's link to reliability and earthly support.

Again, these myths are not about a specific zodiac sign, but they reflect the same broad theme: the bovine figure as a provider of wealth, nourishment, and stable foundation.

Native American Cultures

Across the many Native American cultures, the buffalo or bison sometimes holds a place similar to what the bull represents in Eurasian settings. Though different in species, the concept of a powerful, horned animal feeding the people recurs:

Plains Tribes
For tribes on the Great Plains, the buffalo was crucial for food, clothing, and shelter. Its image often became a cultural symbol of strength, community, and the continuity of life.

Bison vs. Bull
While not the same creature, the bison's role in providing resources carries a parallel to how people in other parts of the world revered the bull for farm work and food.

Ceremonies
Ceremonies and dances might focus on thanking or respecting the buffalo. These do not match up with Western astrology, but they

show a similar respect for a steady, powerful beast that supports human life.

This highlights how different cultures, even those without a direct tradition of Taurus, honor large grazing animals for the security they bring.

African Views of Bulls and Cattle

Across Africa, cattle ownership has often been a sign of wealth and social standing. Various groups have strong traditions around livestock:

Masai Culture (East Africa)
Cattle are central to Masai identity. The bull can represent leadership or wealth. While this is not about Taurus astrology, the reverence for a strong bull in the herd resonates with the idea of dependable power.

Zulu Traditions
Some ceremonies might involve cattle, with the bull playing a role in blessings or transitions. This again points to themes of fertility, stability, and providing resources.

Art and Symbolism
Across different African regions, cave paintings or carvings sometimes depict bulls in ways that signal their importance. Though not a zodiac sign, the symbolism remains consistent: strength, nourishment, and a link to the earth.

South American Connections

In South America, the bull might not be as widely featured in ancient indigenous traditions as other animals, but contact with Spanish culture brought bull-related customs:

Andean Regions
Llamas and alpacas took precedence in some highland areas, yet cattle introduced by Europeans became a part of local life, leading to ranching traditions.

Festival Scenes
Spanish-influenced bull events (like bull runs or bullfights) spread to parts of the continent. While controversial from an animal-rights view, they highlight the bull's role as a powerful figure to be respected or confronted.

Symbol of Ranching
Countries like Argentina, with large cattle ranches, tie the bull or steer to national identity. The Gaucho culture focuses on horsemanship and cattle rearing, once more linking the bull to steadfast labor and strength.

This mixture of local heritage and colonial influence created an environment where bull symbolism can show up in ranching traditions, echoing themes of reliability and power in daily life.

Modern Global Interpretations of Taurus

In today's world, the idea of Taurus from Western astrology has traveled far, thanks to media, the internet, and cultural exchange. People in places where the zodiac was not historically dominant might still read Western horoscopes or identify with a sign, Taurus included.

Pop Culture Spread
Newspapers, magazines, and websites share daily or monthly horoscopes. Taurus is typically described as stable, stubborn, and appreciative of comfort. This uniform portrayal can overshadow local astrological systems.

Fusion with Local Beliefs
Some individuals blend Western zodiac insights with their region's spiritual or astrological traditions, creating a personalized worldview.

Tattoo and Fashion Trends
Taurus symbols, like the bull's head or the glyph (circle with horns), appear in tattoos or jewelry. People adopt them for personal reasons, sometimes beyond astrology, simply because they like the bull's representation of power or perseverance.

Thus, modern global culture has a tapestry of bull symbolism, with Taurus from Western astrology mingling among various local ideas about strong, horned animals and what they stand for.

Common Themes Across Cultures

Throughout these various cultures and timelines, we can see certain recurring themes about the bull or bull-like symbols:

Stability and Earth Connection
Whether it is the farmland bull or a mythical creature in a story, these animals often stand for grounded, reliable energy.

Fertility and Prosperity
Many societies link the bull to the land's fruitfulness and to wealth (often measured by livestock). This can parallel Taurus traits of seeking security and nurturing growth.

Patience and Strength
Bulls are patient in the field, yet immensely strong when provoked. Taurus is often described similarly: calm, but forceful if pushed too far.

Provider of Food and Resources
From the Great Plains bison to the bull in ancient Egypt, these animals often feed or clothe the people, connecting them to the basics of survival—mirroring Taurus's focus on the tangible, physical side of life.

While each culture's stories differ, these themes show a consistent respect for the bull's calm yet powerful presence, which lines up with the typical depiction of Taurus.

How Cultural Ideas May Reflect in a Taurus Person

Though a modern Taurus might not directly link themselves to ancient bulls or rituals, these historical and cultural ideas can resonate in subtle ways:

Desire for Security: As many cultures prized cattle as wealth, Taurus might similarly prize job stability, a home they can rely on, and a steady routine.

Calm Power: Bulls are not frantic unless threatened. A Taurus personality often mirrors this, showing patience and slow movement but strong will if pushed.

Practical Grounding: Bulls labor on the earth, and Taurus tends to keep a practical mindset about daily life, focusing on real-world results and comfort.

Looking at these parallels can deepen a Taurus individual's sense of identity, seeing that their traits reflect a longstanding human respect for the bull's dependable force.

Celebrations and Festivals

Many cultures have or had special events related to bulls—some joyous, some solemn. For instance, we can mention:

Running of the Bulls (Spain)
A well-known event. People run in front of bulls through town streets. While this does not directly connect to Taurus the zodiac, it highlights how bulls can symbolize both excitement and risk.

Harvest Gatherings
In some agricultural traditions, bulls or oxen were honored at harvest time, recognizing their role in plowing fields or hauling crops.

Local Fair Traditions
In parts of Asia or Africa, fairs might show prized cattle or have bull contests. This can be a time when the community admires the animals' strength.

These cultural occasions show that the bull's importance goes beyond just a star sign—people have long had reasons to honor the bull's contribution to daily life.

Modern Astrology Discussions in Different Countries

Nowadays, people globally read about their sun sign, including Taurus. Yet, how deeply they accept or use that information can differ by place and culture:

Europe and the Americas
Western astrology is widespread. Taurus individuals might read daily horoscopes, watch online videos, or consult an astrologer.

Asia
East Asian countries have their own zodiac systems, but some folks

still take an interest in Western astrology. A person might say, "I am a Taurus, but also a Rabbit in the Chinese zodiac," combining both.

Africa and the Middle East
Western horoscopes are available through media or the internet, though local beliefs or religions may shape how seriously people treat them.

Mixing Traditions
Some people use elements from multiple systems—for instance, exploring Vedic astrology to compare it with Western zodiac insights for Taurus.

This modern blending shows how the idea of Taurus can pop up in many corners of the globe, sometimes coexisting with older local symbols of the bull.

Studying Taurus-Like Qualities in Cultural Heroes

In stories, heroes or gods sometimes show traits we might call "Taurus-like" even if they have no direct link to the zodiac sign:

Strong Silent Types
Many cultures' mythic heroes are patient, unshakeable, and not quick to brag, reminiscent of Taurus's calm. They often do what must be done, step by step.

Fertility and Growth
Some figures watch over farmland or forests, encouraging the abundance of nature. Taurus's association with growth is echoed here.

Keeper of Traditions
Legends about figures who maintain the old ways and resist hasty changes can remind us of Taurus's preference for stability.

Protectors of the Land

In certain tales, a bull-like character or a sturdy hero defends the community's resources. This speaks to the protective aspect of Taurus, ensuring safety for themselves and others.

Such parallels help us see that the "Taurus spirit"—steadfast, grounded, caring for the earth—can emerge in many cultural narratives, even without mentioning astrology.

Respecting Cultural Differences

While it can be fun to compare how different societies view the bull or traits like stability, it is also vital to respect that each culture has its own context. For example:

- A Celtic bull symbol might have a spiritual meaning that is not exactly the same as Taurus's astrological portrayal.

- The Chinese Ox year stands for certain qualities, but it is not a direct match to Taurus's sun sign period.

- African bull traditions might revolve around local harvest rhythms, having nothing to do with star charts.

Recognizing these distinctions can prevent oversimplifying. Taurus from Western astrology is a system with particular rules and symbolism, coexisting alongside many other cultural viewpoints on bulls.

Traveling the World as a Taurus

A Taurus interested in how cultures celebrate or admire the bull could:

Visit Ancient Sites
Places like Crete (with Minoan ruins) or Egypt (temples that honored Apis the bull) might appeal to a Taurus's sense of historical groundedness.

Attend Local Markets
Seeing how cattle, produce, and other goods are handled can show the region's connection to the land. Taurus might appreciate the calm process of walking through markets.

Learn Local Bull-Related Customs
Whether it is a festival or a small rural practice, discovering how locals treat cattle or bulls can open the Taurus perspective on how universal the bull's image is.

Reflect on Common Themes
Observing how different people see the bull as powerful, comforting, or essential might deepen a Taurus traveler's appreciation for the sign's universal presence.

This approach can enrich a Taurus's global experiences, connecting them with the symbolism that resonates with their own core traits.

The Future of Taurus Symbolism

As the world keeps changing, how might the bull's imagery or Taurus concepts shift?

Sustainability Movements
With growing interest in eco-friendly living, bulls or cattle might spark debates about farming methods or environmental impacts. Taurus's earth focus could link with concerns about land preservation, mindful resource use, and stable ecosystems.

Cultural Exchange
More people may blend Western astrology with their native beliefs, giving rise to new interpretations of Taurus that combine local bull symbols with the traditional zodiac.

Technological Influence
As digital tools transform how we think about identity, Taurus traits might show up in online communities or virtual reality platforms, with the bull symbol used in creative digital ways.

Preserving Traditions
Groups aiming to keep ancient customs alive might continue passing down bull-related stories or rituals, ensuring the link between the bull and stability remains in cultural memory.

In these ways, the Taurus figure will likely stay relevant, evolving with each new era and cultural perspective.

CHAPTER 17: TAURUS IN ART AND STORIES

The symbol of the bull is widespread in many forms of art and storytelling. In literature, paintings, sculptures, and even modern films or shows, the bull often appears as a figure of strength, patience, or earthy power. Since Taurus is represented by the bull in Western astrology, we can find parallels between Taurus traits and how bulls are depicted across the creative world. In this chapter, we will explore how the bull or bull-like characters show up in art and stories, consider what themes they convey, and link these themes back to the energy we often connect with Taurus. We will also look at ways modern artists continue to draw on the bull's image, sometimes referencing Taurus directly.

Early Cave Paintings and Ancient Art

Artistic depictions of the bull go back thousands of years. One of the earliest forms of human creativity involves images of animals on cave walls:

Cave of Lascaux (France)
 The famous cave paintings include large bulls among other animals. While these are not about the zodiac, they show that humans have long been fascinated with the bull's strong form. It is believed such art could be tied to rituals or respect for the animal's power.

Mesopotamian Carvings
 Ancient Mesopotamian sculptures and reliefs sometimes show powerful bulls. They could be guardians at the gates of cities or temples. These colossal figures mirror the idea of the bull as a

steadfast protector—much like Taurus is often seen as a stable presence.

Egyptian Temples and Tombs
Bull representations, like the Apis bull, often appear in temple art. The meticulous style of Egyptian carving and painting reveals a reverence for the bull's presence, akin to a spiritual or royal embodiment of stability and fertility.

Even from these earliest examples, we see artists using the bull to convey admiration for endurance and grounded power—traits we commonly link with Taurus.

The Minoan Bull-Leaping Frescoes

One of the most famous pieces of bull-related art from ancient times is the Minoan bull-leaping fresco found on the island of Crete:

Fresco Content
The artwork shows figures jumping or vaulting over the back of a charging bull. It is colorful, dynamic, and highlights the bull's central place in Minoan culture.

Symbolic Meaning
While scholars debate the exact meaning, many suggest it was a ritual or sport that showcased the bull's strength and people's skill and bravery. This again fits the dual nature of the bull: potentially dangerous but also valued.

Link to Taurus
Though these frescoes are not labeled "Taurus," they emphasize the bull's grace, power, and connection to cultural identity. Modern interpretations might see echoes of Taurus's steady energy and the careful interplay between human skill and nature's force.

These Minoan images demonstrate how the bull has been an inspiration for dynamic, vivid art, underlining its importance in ancient societies.

Greek and Roman Myths in Art

Moving from ancient civilizations to classical Greece and Rome, we find many sculptures, mosaics, and paintings referencing mythic bulls, including those that later informed Western zodiac ideas:

Europa and the Bull
Artists from antiquity up to the Renaissance and beyond have painted the story of Zeus taking bull form to carry Europa away. The bull is often shown as regal, calm, yet powerful—an image easily linked to Taurus-like themes of quiet strength.

The Cretan Bull
Another mythic figure is the Cretan Bull, which Heracles (Hercules) had to capture as one of his Twelve Labors. Art depicting this challenge often shows Hercules wrestling the bull, stressing its raw power.

Roman Frescoes and Mosaics
Romans inherited Greek myths, so bull imagery continued in villas and public buildings. Sometimes, the bull would be featured simply for its strong presence, other times to illustrate mythic scenes.

These artistic pieces spread the idea that the bull was both majestic and not to be taken lightly—much like how Taurus is often viewed as dependable but strong-willed.

The Renaissance to Modern Western Art

As Europe shifted into the Renaissance and later periods, the bull remained a symbol in paintings and sculptures, though sometimes with changing or added meanings:

Biblical and Religious Themes
Scenes from Christian texts might include the golden calf or sacrificial bulls, reflecting moral lessons about devotion or sin. Artists like Raphael or Caravaggio occasionally portrayed these moments with intense emotion.

Allegorical Paintings
Some Renaissance or Baroque artists used the bull as an allegory for certain human qualities, like stubbornness, nobility, or fertility. Though less direct, these interpretations can be seen as variations of Taurus traits—steadfastness or ties to earthly abundance.

Picasso's Bulls
In the 20th century, artist Pablo Picasso famously used the bull image in his works, including the iconic "Guernica," where the bull can represent various themes, such as the Spanish people's spirit or broader human suffering. Picasso also created many bull-related sketches and sculptures. While not a direct sign of Taurus, the bull in his art symbolizes strength, sometimes overshadowed by turmoil.

Salvador Dalí and Surrealism
Another Spanish artist, Dalí, sometimes inserted bull imagery into dreamlike scenes, giving a surreal twist to the standard ideas of bulls as symbols of raw force or persistence.

In each of these examples, the bull stands for more than just a farm animal—it carries layered meanings of resilience, power, or even spiritual or emotional conflict, echoing qualities we link to Taurus's solidity and inner intensity.

Artistic Depictions in Other Regions

While Europe is well-known for classical and modern bull art, other regions also have prominent pieces:

China and the Ox
Chinese paintings may feature the Ox in pastoral scenes or New Year pictures. These images often symbolize diligence, calm strength, and harmony with the land—reflecting traits that parallel Taurus.

India's Nandi in Sculpture
Statues of Nandi, the sacred bull of Lord Shiva, appear in temples across India. The artistry in these sculptures—sometimes large, sometimes small—emphasizes devotion, patience, and a protective stance.

Middle Eastern Crafts
Traditional crafts might include bull motifs in patterns or designs, especially in regions once influenced by Mesopotamia. These can appear on fabrics, ceramics, or carvings, again hinting at stable power and cultural heritage.

From Asia to the Middle East, the bull's image remains a favorite subject, aligning well with themes of diligence, fertility, or spiritual grounding.

Literature and Folklore Featuring Bulls

Beyond visual art, bulls also show up in written stories and folklore, sometimes with a personality or role that hints at Taurus's calm but determined nature:

Irish Myth: The Cattle Raid of Cooley
This epic centers on the Donn Cuailnge, a prized bull, and the entire

conflict of the story revolves around capturing it. While not described as "Taurus," the bull's significance is tied to status and power.

Fables and Fairy Tales
In various European folk stories, a bull might help a hero plow a field or guide them, reinforcing a notion of loyalty or quiet strength.

Modern Novels
Contemporary literature might include bull characters or bull-themed metaphors to show someone's unwavering focus. Authors sometimes employ the bull motif to illustrate a character's stubbornness or fidelity.

These written works expand the bull's presence into narratives that highlight both the positive (loyal, reliable) and challenging (stubborn, formidable) sides that align with typical Taurus traits.

Films and Media Portrayals

Movies, TV shows, and animated features also use bull or bull-like characters to represent certain qualities:

"Ferdinand" (Film)
Adapted from a children's book, Ferdinand is a bull with a gentle spirit. He is large and strong but prefers peace over fighting—an approach that closely matches the Taurus reputation for calmness unless provoked.

Western Films
Bulls or steers sometimes appear in ranch scenes, symbolizing the rugged side of life on the range. These depictions can again underscore how the bull stands for strength and the challenges of taming nature—echoing Taurus's elemental ties to the earth.

Symbolic Use in Animated or Fantasy Media
Some fantasy settings include minotaur-like creatures: half-human, half-bull beings. While these are more mythical, they typically show cunning or brute force, reminding us that the bull is viewed as a powerful presence.

In these media, the bull often comes with traits of loyalty, might, a certain reluctance to fight unless needed, or steadfastness—much like the steadfast core people associate with Taurus.

Bullfighting as a Cultural Phenomenon

While controversial, bullfighting in countries like Spain or parts of Latin America has also influenced art and stories:

Posters and Paintings
Colorful bullfight posters have become iconic, showing a proud bull facing a matador. Artists like Picasso and others have created works referencing these events, using the bull to symbolize life's struggle.

Poems and Novels
Writers such as Ernest Hemingway, in works like "Death in the Afternoon," explored the emotional side of bullfighting. The bull is seen as brave and noble, forced into a tragic dance.

Taurus Reflections
In a metaphorical sense, some see the bull's role in the ring as representing calm stoicism turned into a fight when cornered, paralleling how a Taurus might respond if severely provoked—usually peaceful but strong in defense.

Though bullfighting may be viewed differently by various audiences, its portrayal in art has helped cement the bull's image as dignified yet capable of fierce resistance when forced.

Modern Advertising and Branding

Bulls appear in logos or product mascots, playing on the bull's link to strength and reliability:

Financial Industry
The famous bull statue at Wall Street in New York is meant to symbolize market prosperity and upward momentum, commonly called a "bull market." This resonates with Taurus's association with growth and security.

Energy Drinks and Sports Teams
Brands sometimes use the bull or bull head to suggest power, energy, or unstoppable drive—qualities they hope customers will associate with their product.

Consumer Confidence
Some companies use a bull in ads to show consistency or trust, hinting at a stable, dependable product—qualities that again reflect Taurus-like values.

This commercial use of bull imagery helps spread the idea that the bull stands for unyielding strength and can be relied upon to deliver results.

Bulls in Children's Books and Tales

Many children's stories worldwide feature a bull as a kind or gentle helper, or as a fierce beast with a hidden soft side:

The Story of Ferdinand
Illustrates how a bull can be sweet and loving flowers, opposing the standard idea of aggression—a message of peacefulness.

Picture Books in Various Languages
Bulls or oxen might serve as farm friends teaching lessons about

cooperation, patience, or hard work, reinforcing a link to traits of calm and diligence.

Moral Lessons
Some children's tales use the bull to show that external strength can pair with an inner desire for harmony, sending a message that physical power does not always mean recklessness. This resonates with the Taurus mindset of balance between strength and stability.

Artistic Interpretations of Taurus Specifically

Apart from general bull art, some modern artists create pieces referring explicitly to the zodiac sign Taurus:

Zodiac Collections
Illustrators or designers might produce a series of artworks, each dedicated to a zodiac sign. The Taurus piece often features a bull's head with symbols of nature or abundance, highlighting Taurus's earthy side.

Digital Art and Astrology Channels
Online creators can share stylized Taurus designs, mixing cosmic or star themes with a bull image. These works often emphasize the sign's calm and serene aura, using muted greens or browns to evoke the earth element.

Contemporary Sculptures
Some modern sculptors might craft an abstract bull form titled "Taurus," merging the timeless power of the bull with sleek, updated lines or materials. These pieces can appear in galleries or public spaces, linking age-old symbolism with modern expression.

Such works bring Taurus directly into artistic conversation, highlighting the zodiac's cultural presence.

Themes and Symbols Often Paired with Bulls in Art

When artists add a bull to their work, certain images or themes might appear together:

Flowers or Greenery
A bull surrounded by lush fields can show fertility, growth, or harmony with nature—matching Taurus's earth element.

Tactile Textures
Many bull depictions use thick brushstrokes or strong lines to capture the creature's physicality, echoing the solid essence of Taurus.

Earthy Colors
Browns, greens, or golds often appear in bull art. Warm, grounded tones can reflect Taurus's comfort with the land and home environment.

Patterns of Circles or Horn-Like Shapes
Horns might be stylized into swirling shapes, giving the art an energetic yet stable quality.

By noticing these repeated themes, we see how artists naturally link the bull image to strength, nature, and dependable presence—Taurus hallmarks.

Contrasts in Depiction: Aggressive vs. Serene

One interesting point is that bulls can be shown as raging beasts or calm, nurturing animals:

Aggressive Representations
Some works highlight the bull's charge or anger, suggesting chaos or danger. This might parallel how a Taurus can become unyielding if badly provoked.

Serene Depictions
Others show the bull grazing peacefully, offering a sense of tranquility and patience, mirroring Taurus's usual calm demeanor.

Dual Nature
Artists might combine both: the bull stands quietly, but its muscles are tense, implying latent power. This duality aligns closely with Taurus, known for being peace-loving but having a strong backbone when pushed.

Thus, art often captures both sides of Taurus's nature: the usual calm and, beneath it, the capacity for force if cornered.

Story Archetypes Matching Taurus

In stories, certain character archetypes reflect the bull's or Taurus's qualities:

The Reliable Companion
A steady friend who may not talk much but is always there in times of need. This character might be physically strong and protective.

The Farmer or Craftsman
A patient worker who takes pride in building or growing things slowly. Plot lines may revolve around their dedication paying off.

The Quiet Protector
Someone who stands back until danger arrives, then uses great power to defend loved ones. This mirrors the bull's typical calm until threatened.

The Reluctant Fighter
A character who is forced into conflict but would rather live peacefully—again, reminiscent of how many see Taurus.

In reading or watching these characters, we can catch glimpses of Taurus's steady, sometimes stubborn presence that anchors a story.

Creative Expressions for Taurus Individuals

For someone born under Taurus, certain art forms might appeal especially strongly because they allow for slow, methodical process and tangible results:

Sculpture or Pottery
Shaping clay or carving stone could suit Taurus's tactile sense. They can watch form emerge step by step, enjoying physical craftsmanship.

Realistic Drawing or Painting
Many Taurus individuals like the detail-oriented aspect of rendering nature scenes, still lifes, or portraits with careful attention.

Garden or Land Art
Designing flowerbeds, rock gardens, or small landscape setups can blend artistry with a love for the earth.

Storytelling Rooted in Daily Life
Taurus authors might write short stories or novels about everyday folks and how they grow step by step, focusing on realistic detail and emotional grounding.

Such creative expressions let Taurus delve into art and stories while staying connected to their preference for practical, grounded processes.

Festivals Celebrating Art and the Bull

Some modern events bring together bull symbolism and creative displays:

Bull-Themed Exhibitions
Museums might host shows on the history of bull depictions, collecting ancient artifacts, paintings, and modern installations. Visitors can trace how the bull's image evolved over centuries.

Cultural Festivals
In regions where bulls have historical significance—like certain parts of Spain, Greece, or India—festivals may display artworks or dance performances that pay tribute to the bull's heritage.

Sculptural Trails
Some cities create art trails featuring bull or cattle statues designed by different artists. People visit each statue around town, each with a unique design, merging community fun with a shared theme of stability or tradition.

At these events, attendees often discover how flexible and varied bull imagery can be, reflecting both the past and the present.

The Bull in Digital and Virtual Art

As technology grows, new forms of art emerge, and the bull remains a favored figure in modern, virtual spaces:

Digital Paintings
Artists create complex, layered images of bulls using software, experimenting with color and texture in ways traditional media cannot.

3D Models and Animation
In video games or animated films, a bull might be rendered in high detail, showing realistic fur, muscle movements, and expressive features—sometimes directly referencing Taurus or a bull persona.

Augmented Reality and NFTs
Some creators use AR or NFT platforms to share bull-themed art. Collectors or fans can view or own a unique bull representation in a digital format, reflecting how cultural symbols keep evolving with technology.

Even in these high-tech forms, the bull's essence—steady strength—persists, suggesting that the core of Taurus continues to inspire fresh mediums.

Life Lessons from Bull Art and Stories

Whether in ancient frescos or modern films, the bull teaches certain lessons that can resonate with Taurus or anyone who appreciates these qualities:

Balance of Peace and Power
The bull is typically calm but can show enormous force if challenged. This duality can remind viewers of the importance of boundaries and the value of peaceful living until action is required.

Steady Progress
Many works depict the bull as unhurried, representing patience and persistence. This can inspire people to handle life's tasks one step at a time.

Connection to the Earth
Bulls graze, plow fields, or stand in lush pastures. This imagery can prompt reflection on caring for the land, respecting nature's rhythms—an idea central to Taurus's earthy sensibilities.

Stability and Reliability
Repeatedly, stories show a bull's unwavering stance or loyalty. A bull

might become a symbol of protection or a steady resource, echoing Taurus's role in friendships or workplaces.

Through encountering bull-inspired art or tales, we gain insight into why Taurus is famed for reliability and calm, learning to appreciate these traits in ourselves or those around us.

Encouraging Artistic Exploration for Taurus

If you are a Taurus or know someone who is, here are ways to deepen the connection with bull-themed art and stories:

Visit Museums with Bull Exhibits
Seek out any special showcases about bulls or check sections featuring ancient Mesopotamian, Greek, or Egyptian art.

Explore Local Culture
If your region has bull-related traditions, attend events or read up on the stories behind them. This can spark creativity or help you feel closer to Taurus imagery.

Try Creative Projects
Consider painting or sketching a bull, creating a short story with a bull character, or even crafting a small bull sculpture. Engaging directly in art can be both relaxing and insightful.

Study Mythic Tales
Look at myths from around the world that feature bulls or bull-like beings. Compare how they line up with your understanding of Taurus qualities.

CHAPTER 18: TAURUS OVER TIME

Taurus has been recognized for many centuries, going back to the ancient period when civilizations started to chart the stars and name the constellations. Over this long stretch of history, the way people view Taurus has changed in various ways. Ideas once connected with myth and religion slowly evolved, passing through medieval thought, Renaissance discovery, and modern scientific debate. The core themes of the sign—steadiness, reliability, and a link to the earth—have remained, yet different times added unique perspectives.

In this chapter, we will look at how Taurus was understood in different historical periods, moving from the early days of astrology through medieval and Renaissance times, and on to the modern era. We will see how influences such as scientific shifts, cultural changes, and new attitudes about astrology have all shaped the meaning of Taurus. By exploring these transformations, we can better understand Taurus's role in society and how people from diverse generations have adopted or adapted this sign's traits into their beliefs.

Ancient Roots and Early Babylonian Influence

Many link Western astrology's early development to Mesopotamia and Babylon, where star-watching was serious business. Back then, people measured and recorded planet movements, naming constellations that included the group of stars we now call Taurus.

Star Catalogs and Constellation Myths
The Babylonians had a remarkable knowledge of the sky, creating star lists that placed a bull shape in that region. These lists influenced Greek scholars, who connected the dots to form the Taurus constellation.

Agricultural Links
In these ancient societies, bulls were vital for plowing and a secure harvest. Some historians believe that identifying a "Bull of Heaven" in the sky might have been a way to honor the real bulls on Earth, highlighting stability and abundance—two ideas that line up with how many see Taurus today.

Movement to Greece and Rome
Over time, Mesopotamian star knowledge traveled into Greek culture. Greek writers shaped this into the myth of Zeus transforming into a bull, which later carried through to the Roman era. That mythic lens gave Taurus a divine or grand flavor, emphasizing power and presence.

Thus, the earliest understanding of Taurus heavily connected to practical life (crops, farm work) and to spiritual awe (the bull's cosmic significance), blending real and mythic views.

Hellenistic Period and the Formalization of Zodiac Signs

Moving from Babylonian ideas, Greek scholars in the Hellenistic period gave us a more structured form of astrology. This era (roughly 323–31 BCE) saw major growth in astrological theories, setting a lasting pattern for the zodiac system.

Systematizing the Zodiac
Greek thinkers, building on Mesopotamian data, established the 12-sign format we know. Taurus became fixed as the second sign,

following Aries. This spot in the zodiac wheel linked Taurus to certain months in spring and to an earth-based temperament.

Philosophical Views
Philosophers like Aristotle pondered the nature of elements—earth, water, air, and fire—helping set the idea that Taurus is an earth sign. Taurus's persistent, stable qualities were often admired as part of a balanced personality.

Rise of Personal Horoscopes
While earlier astrology tracked events for entire kingdoms, the Hellenistic era refined personal birth charts. People began saying, "I was born under Taurus," tying personal traits to the bull sign.

Blend of Myth and Observation
The Greek practice of associating constellations with gods blended mythic stories like Europa and the Bull with real star patterns. Taurus became more than a symbol of farmland—it also reflected a cosmic or divine bull presence.

By this point, Taurus was firmly rooted in astrology, described as a patient, strong, and consistent sign symbolized by the bull, honored in both everyday and celestial contexts.

Roman Empire and Spread Across Europe

As Rome expanded, it carried Greek-influenced astrology throughout Europe. Astrological practice became accessible to broader groups, from elite scholars to ordinary believers.

Roman Adaptation
The Romans renamed Greek gods but kept the same zodiac framework. Taurus's meaning remained similar: an earth sign seen as stable and physically grounded.

Connection with Roman Religion
Certain Roman festivals might hint at the bull's symbolic presence. Though these were not purely about Taurus, the cultural environment kept bull imagery alive—whether for sacrifice, ceremony, or art.

Astrology in the Empire
Many Romans believed in personal horoscopes. Records show emperors consulting astrologers for guidance. Taurus, known for reliability, could be viewed favorably if an emperor sought steady supporters or wise counsels.

Influence on Provinces
As Roman roads and ideas spread, so did zodiac knowledge. Provinces learned about the 12 signs, including Taurus, merging local beliefs with the new cosmic system. This mix further shaped how Taurus was understood, sometimes fusing with older bull worship traditions in distant regions.

Thus, by the end of the Roman Empire, astrology—and Taurus—had begun weaving itself into the cultural tapestry of Europe and the Mediterranean world.

Medieval Interpretations

Following Rome's fall, the medieval period in Europe saw astrology either embraced or questioned, depending on local rulers and religious views. Despite ups and downs, Taurus kept a place in astrological writings.

Influence of Arabic and Persian Scholars
Medieval Europe rediscovered much of Greek and Roman knowledge through Arabic translations. Astrological texts passed through the Islamic world, which had its own robust tradition of star

studies. Writers like al-Biruni and Avicenna might reference the bull sign.

Christian Kingdoms and Astrology

Officially, some church authorities frowned on astrology, wary of predicting the future or attributing too much power to stars. Still, many nobles and scholars secretly studied horoscopes. Taurus, as a sign, was often linked to spring's stable energies—less controversial than more dramatic signs.

Zodiac Imagery in Manuscripts

Illuminated manuscripts often featured each zodiac sign in decorative letters or margins. Taurus might appear as a stylized bull, calmly gazing among blossoms, emphasizing spring renewal.

Practical Use

Farmers in medieval Europe might track astrological calendars, planting seeds or harvesting under specific signs. Taurus's time, in April–May, was prime for sowing and ensuring the land's fertility, linking the sign with growth and a stable cycle of life.

So, in medieval times, Taurus continued to represent the steady heartbeat of agriculture and mild spring energy, even as religion and shifting politics changed the broader context.

Renaissance Astrology and Art

The Renaissance (14th–17th centuries) revived interest in classical knowledge. Astrological thought flourished, especially among intellectuals trying to balance science, philosophy, and art. Taurus found a new stage.

Humanism and the Zodiac

Renaissance thinkers revisited Greek texts in the original language. They combined these with newly popular humanist ideals, reaffirming the zodiac, Taurus included, as a valuable symbolic tool for understanding personality.

Great Artists and Zodiac Depictions

Painters such as Botticelli, Raphael, or later, the Baroque masters, sometimes included zodiac symbols in religious or allegorical works. Taurus might be placed in a corner of a fresco or on a ceiling painting charting the heavens.

Printed Horoscopes

With the printing press, astrological almanacs circulated widely. Taurus's traits—steady, dependable, fond of comforts—reached more readers. Some Renaissance astrologers wrote specifically about how each sign influenced health, romance, or daily living.

Early Scientific Questions

The Renaissance also planted seeds of scientific inquiry that would later challenge astrology. Figures like Copernicus, Galileo, and Kepler studied the cosmos differently. Kepler, for instance, re-examined astrology's mathematics. While these new approaches did not end interest in the sign of Taurus, they led to debates over the zodiac's validity.

Nevertheless, the Renaissance represented a high point of cultural astrology in Europe, where Taurus shone as a symbol of earthy grace, stability, and a well-ordered universe.

Enlightenment to the 19th Century

After the Renaissance, the Enlightenment (late 17th–18th centuries) emphasized reason and scientific progress, often clashing with astrological beliefs. Taurus was not immune to these shifting attitudes.

Rise of Rationalism

Many Enlightenment thinkers dismissed astrology as superstition. Focus turned to observable data. This meant less official support for zodiac lore, including Taurus.

Popular vs. Intellectual Circles

Among the common population, interest in horoscopes often stayed alive, passed down through almanacs. Taurus kept its reputation for calm reliability, though intellectual elites might have scoffed.

Romantic Era Rediscovery

In the 19th century, Romanticism renewed an interest in nature and mystical perspectives. Poets or artists might refer to the zodiac for symbolic reasons. Taurus, with its earthy link, fit Romantic themes of pastoral life and gentle strength.

Slow Scientific Challenges

Astronomy advanced rapidly, revealing more about planets. The gap between scientific astronomy and astrology widened. Yet many still found personal meaning in signs like Taurus—valuing the sense of identity or cosmic connection.

By the late 19th century, Taurus had gone from a mainstream worldview to a more private or popular curiosity, but it never vanished. Instead, it quietly endured among those who cherished symbolic or mystical traditions.

20th-Century Rebirth of Astrology

The 20th century saw a major revival of astrology in Western societies, sometimes called the "New Age" movement. Taurus re-entered public discussions, from newspaper horoscopes to serious astrological study.

New Age Thinking
In the 1960s and 1970s, alternative spiritual movements flourished. Astrology, including the concept of Taurus, gained a fresh audience seeking personal insight outside standard religion.

Media Horoscopes
Newspapers began printing daily or weekly zodiac columns. Taurus was often described as the dependable sign who appreciates comfort, good food, and stability. This simplified portrayal, while popular, reinforced certain stereotypes.

Psychological Astrology
Astrologers like Dane Rudhyar and Liz Greene approached the zodiac with a Jungian or psychological angle. Taurus was presented as embodying basic security needs, the value of routines, and a deep sense of self-worth.

Emergence of "Sun-Sign Astrology"
This was the idea that one's main identity is tied to the sun's position—Taurus in April–May—without delving into full birth charts. Though simplified, it made sign-based astrology more accessible, raising Taurus's profile among casual readers.

In short, the 20th century turned Taurus into a household concept, recognized by millions as the sign of calm, earthy, comfort-seeking individuals, often repeated in magazines and new spiritual circles alike.

The Internet Age and Taurus Today

With the rise of the internet in the late 20th century and beyond, astrology found new platforms. Taurus quickly became a favorite topic in online communities, social media, and digital content.

Online Horoscopes and Blogs
Websites offering daily or monthly forecasts expanded. Taurus folks could read about how the current planetary transits affect their sign—like a cosmic weather report.

Social Media Memes
Social platforms made it easy to share comedic or motivational images about Taurus traits: being stubborn, loving good food, or needing a comfy blanket. This playful side of Taurus spread widely, shaping public perception.

Astro-Influencers
Some individuals built large online followings by posting about astrology. They often described Taurus as the sign that loves relaxation, stable routines, and quality items. This gave Taurus both comedic and warm portrayal in modern pop culture.

Mobile Apps and Personalized Data
Apps emerged that deliver tailored readings, inviting users to explore a deeper birth chart. Here, Taurus could be a sun sign, moon sign, or rising sign. Each variation offered more nuanced insight than typical media horoscopes.

Currently, thanks to digital tools, Taurus is recognized globally by people who may or may not believe in astrology fully. The sign's identity as grounded, comfort-loving, and gentle but firm has become a standard reference point.

Evolving Scientific Critique

While astrology has fans, modern science largely views it with skepticism. Here is how that affects Taurus:

Tests and Experiments
Attempts to prove or disprove astrology typically fail to find

empirical support. Critics say no consistent link exists between birth sign (like Taurus) and personality.

People Separating Fun from Fact
Many treat astrology as entertainment or symbolic language rather than strict science. Taurus thus becomes a "theme" or lens for personal reflection, not a proven cause of behavior.

Psychological Explanations
Some psychologists say we adopt traits we read about in our sign's description if we find them appealing. So, a Taurus might identify more with patience because they want to fit that image.

Longevity Despite Doubt
Even with scientific critique, Taurus remains popular. People find value in the sign's earthy metaphor—an anchor in a fast-changing world, reminding them to slow down and enjoy life's steady rhythms.

So, while no firm scientific backing exists, Taurus endures as a cultural and personal reference, cherished for its symbolic meaning.

The Impact of Cultural Shifts on Taurus Traits

As society changes, so do the ways we describe Taurus. Certain traits remain, but their emphasis shifts:

Comfort and Security in an Era of Uncertainty
Modern times can feel chaotic—technology changes quickly, and global challenges arise. A focus on Taurus's desire for stability might become more relevant, as people yearn for calm in a hectic world.

Environmental Awareness
Many younger generations care about ecological issues. Taurus's earth sign identity can resonate, representing a closeness to nature and an eco-friendly mindset.

Money and Material Comfort
Since finances and security are big concerns, some see Taurus's link to practical matters as either helpful or cautionary—balancing enjoying comforts with responsible spending.

Work-Life Changes
With more freelance or remote jobs, the idea of forming stable daily routines at home might align well with Taurus's preference for predictable schedules and comfortable surroundings.

Thus, Taurus evolves alongside our culture, reflecting how individuals keep blending age-old sign traits with new concerns about work, money, technology, or the planet.

Generational Observations of Taurus

In modern astrology, some talk about how each generation expresses its Taurus side differently:

Baby Boomers (1946–1964)
Known for establishing steady careers. A Taurus boomer might have used their patient drive to rise in a company, collecting practical assets along the way.

Generation X (1965–1980)
Often prized independence. A Taurus in Gen X might combine stability with a self-reliant streak, carefully managing finances while exploring personal freedoms.

Millennials (1981–1996)
Facing economic ups and downs, a Taurus millennial might emphasize frugal living, home comforts, and small indulgences as a safe haven in uncertain job markets.

Gen Z (1997–2012) and Younger
Growing up online, a Taurus of this era might use digital tools to build stable routines, working from home or joining global environmental movements, reflecting the earth sign's caretaker vibe.

Of course, these are broad outlines, but they illustrate how the same sign interacts differently with each historical moment's challenges and hopes.

Taurus in Popular Media and Entertainment

Today, Taurus characters sometimes appear in shows, novels, or movies—either stated outright ("I'm a Taurus!") or portrayed with subtle bull-like qualities:

Fictional Taurus Protagonists
Writers might craft a stable, kind main character who rarely wavers, signifying loyalty. They might or might not label them Taurus, but the qualities match.

Reality TV and Celebrities
Some stars openly share their zodiac sign. Taurus celebrities might be known for reliable public images, a calm approach, or strong personal style. Fans link these traits to the sign.

Online Quizzes
Quizzes invite people to see if they match the "typical Taurus." This further cements certain stereotypes (like "Which sign is the biggest foodie?" often points to Taurus).

Spreading an Image
These portrayals, whether comedic or sincere, shape how the general public sees Taurus: laid-back yet stubborn, practical, enjoying life's pleasures—traits that show up in memes or references in everyday conversation.

Tensions Between Tradition and Modern Adaptation

Over time, conflicts can arise between historical Taurus themes and how new generations interpret them:

Old-Fashioned vs. Progressive
Some people feel the sign's emphasis on routine can seem old-fashioned, clashing with rapid social change. Others see it as a healthy anchor in uncertain times.

Materialism vs. Sustainability
Taurus's link to possessions may be criticized in a world focusing on reducing waste. However, a Taurus might argue for quality items that last long, which can be eco-friendly.

Stubbornness vs. Authentic Values
Critics of the sign's stubborn streak might see it as inflexibility. Taurus individuals can reframe it as a commitment to strong principles rather than blind refusal to budge.

Expanding Meanings
Modern astrology encourages a Taurus to explore deeper emotional growth, not just comfort. So, we see a shift from purely material portrayals to deeper psychological insights.

These tensions show that Taurus, like any sign, is not static. The sign's age-old traits are reinterpreted in the light of current social and personal questions.

Spiritual Practices and Taurus Energy

Some modern spiritual communities celebrate Taurus energy for grounding and mindfulness:

Meditation and Earth Element
Workshops or online groups talk about "grounding like Taurus,"

connecting to the Earth. They may guide participants to slow down, breathe, and anchor in the present.

Crystal or Aromatherapy
Taurus is sometimes linked with certain crystals (like emerald or rose quartz) or scents (like patchouli or rose), believed to enhance steadiness or comfort. Though not scientifically proven, many find these symbols uplifting.

Seasonal Ceremonies
During Taurus season (April 20–May 20), some hold gatherings focusing on nature's rebirth. Participants honor the sign's stable, blossoming vibe.

Affirmations
People might recite statements like, "I embrace my steady progress" or "I cherish the earth's gifts," aligning with Taurus's patient, nurturing outlook.

While these practices vary widely, they show how Taurus continues to inspire personal well-being methods that link symbolic ideas to daily self-care.

Cultural Adaptations Across the Globe

With astrology present nearly everywhere, Taurus merges with local traditions in unique ways:

Blend with Eastern Zodiacs
Someone born in the Chinese Year of the Ox might compare those Ox traits to Taurus traits, noticing common ideas of diligence and calm. This cross-cultural approach enriches each system.

Local Festivals
In places that already celebrate the bull for historical reasons, adding a Taurus theme might be seen at astrology fairs or markets.

Social Media Platforms in Different Languages
A Taurus in Brazil, Japan, or Nigeria can share memes or stories about their sign, mixing local humor or references with universal Taurus jokes (like loving to nap, enjoying hearty meals, and so on).

Global Exchange
People from different backgrounds trade experiences about how they express Taurus traits—some focusing on nature, others on family or comfort.

In this sense, the sign keeps evolving, shaped by the diversity of worldwide voices who embrace it.

Continual Debate: "Does Taurus Really Matter?"

Amid all these changes, one question persists: does astrology (and Taurus) genuinely shape people's lives?

Individual Choice
Some folks see Taurus as a symbolic guide, using it to reflect on personal habits. Others see it as entertainment with no real effect.

Ethical Use
Believers often say that acknowledging sign traits should not limit someone or justify negative behavior. For instance, a Taurus should not say, "I'm stubborn because of my sign, so I'll never compromise." Instead, they might strive to use that firmness positively.

A Source of Community
Many enjoy meeting others who share their sign. Taurus groups

might exchange recipes, gardening tips, or self-care routines. Whether it is purely psychological or not, it can foster bonds.

Respecting Skepticism
For those who demand scientific proof, astrology remains unproven. Both perspectives can coexist, as long as believers in Taurus avoid pushing their view as fact onto others.

In the end, "Taurus" endures because it offers a framework that resonates emotionally, symbolically, or socially, even if not scientifically.

Famous Taurus Figures over Time

A quick look at notable people historically or currently associated with Taurus:

William Shakespeare (April 26, 1564)
While birth records from that era can be iffy, tradition places him as a Taurus. Fans point to his deep understanding of human nature and practical insight into daily life.

Queen Elizabeth II (April 21, 1926)
Known for a long, steady reign, often described as stable and dependable—traits linked to Taurus's calm persistence.

Audrey Hepburn (May 4, 1929)
Admired for classic grace, personal style, and a gentle presence that many see as Taurus-like.

Modern Artists and Celebrities
Artists like Adele (May 5, 1988) exhibit strong vocal talent and a grounded persona that fans associate with Taurus's earthy authenticity.

While not every famous Taurus fits the stereotype, these examples show how fans link consistent, patient, or enduring qualities to the sign.

Looking to the Future: Taurus and Coming Trends

In the upcoming decades, as technology and society evolve, Taurus might take on fresh angles:

Virtual Realities and Comfort
Taurus could be seen as the sign that finds stable, cozy virtual spaces—whether in online communities or digital experiences designed for relaxation.

Climate Action
With ongoing environmental concerns, Taurus's earth-centered approach might inspire folks to protect natural resources, tying the sign to green activism.

Slow Living Movements
Trendy ideas like "slow living" or "mindful minimalism" align well with Taurus's patient pace, possibly drawing more people to see the sign as a role model for balanced living.

Continued Global Spread
Astrology is not shrinking; it is spreading through social media. Taurus, as one of the more down-to-earth signs, will likely remain a strong reference for those craving stability.

We can guess that Taurus's emphasis on calm, self-care, and reliability will keep resonating as the world speeds up, giving people a reminder to pause and stay grounded.

Past and Present: What Remains the Same?

Across millennia, certain Taurus features have stayed remarkably stable:

Association with Spring and Growth
In the Northern Hemisphere, Taurus's season aligns with blossoming plants and new life—a timeless link to fertility and comfort.

Bull Symbolism
The bull or bull-like figure consistently shows up in art, myth, or religion, always embodying strength and patience.

Practical, Down-to-Earth Attitude
Whether in Babylonian farmland or modern city life, Taurus is depicted as focusing on real tasks, tangible rewards, and trustworthy routines.

Desire for Security
People who identify with Taurus traits usually mention feeling safer with predictability, which resonates through every historical era, from ancient harvest seasons to modern job markets.

These key elements form the backbone of Taurus's identity, uniting ancient star lore with personal feelings in today's technology-driven culture.

CHAPTER 19: TAURUS AND SUITABLE PLACES

For Taurus, environment matters deeply. Many feel calmer and happier in places that echo their love for stability, comfort, and natural beauty. Since Taurus is an earth sign, it often thrives in settings that allow contact with nature, cozy spots to unwind, and practical arrangements for daily routines. However, each Taurus individual may have different preferences based on personal taste, budget, or cultural background.

In this chapter, we will explore what makes a place "suitable" for Taurus, looking at both home environments and travel destinations. We will consider how Taurus might select living spaces, arrange interiors, and find regions of the world that align with the sign's grounded approach. We will also look at how Taurus can navigate busy cities or fast-paced workplaces while preserving their sense of stability. These insights can help Taurus individuals make deliberate choices about where they live, work, and relax, ensuring a better fit for their natural style.

Why Environment Matters to Taurus

All zodiac signs interact with their surroundings in different ways, but for Taurus, the physical environment is particularly influential:

Earth Element Roots
Being an earth sign ties Taurus to tangible reality. If the surroundings feel chaotic—loud, disorganized—Taurus might be unsettled.

Need for Comfort
Taurus typically loves soft textures, warm lighting, and cozy furniture. When the environment meets these needs, a Taurus can fully relax.

Desire for Routine
Living or working in a place with minimal sudden changes can help Taurus feel secure. If the environment shifts constantly, it may bring stress.

Connection to Nature
Many Taurus individuals enjoy nature-based views or at least some greenery. This link to the land can recharge their energy and sense of well-being.

Understanding how deeply environment affects Taurus can guide them in designing a space or choosing a location that supports their calm, practical nature.

Ideal Home Settings

For Taurus, a comfortable home is often a priority. Here are key qualities a Taurus might seek:

Calming Colors and Natural Elements
Soft earthy tones—beiges, greens, muted browns—can make a space feel grounded. Wood furniture, houseplants, or stone accents also bring a sense of the outdoors inside.

Quality Over Quantity
Instead of stuffing a home with many cheap items, a Taurus might invest in fewer pieces that are sturdy and well-made. For example, a solid wooden table or a plush sofa that lasts.

Functional Layout

Taurus values practicality. The home might have easy-to-clean floors, organized kitchen cabinets, and well-labeled storage so they do not waste time searching for things.

Comfortable Spaces to Relax

A Taurus might designate a reading nook with soft blankets or a well-lit corner for crafts. They enjoy cozy spots to wind down after work.

Outdoor Access

If possible, a small garden, patio, or balcony can let Taurus reconnect with plants or fresh air. Even a few pots of herbs near a window can suffice if large outdoor space is not available.

Setting up a home that prioritizes peace, function, and quality helps Taurus maintain that stable feeling day to day.

City vs. Rural Living

When choosing between urban and rural life, Taurus's preferences vary:

Rural Advantages

- Closer to nature, quiet surroundings, and larger yards for gardening.
- Less noise and fewer crowds, which can help a Taurus keep calm.
- Possibly cheaper housing, allowing room for a comfortable home layout.

Rural Challenges

- Limited cultural or work opportunities.

- Longer travel distances for essential shopping or social events.

Urban Advantages

- Access to jobs, cultural events, and a wide range of services or restaurants.
- Shopping for high-quality items becomes easier in a big city.
- Many neighborhoods can be safe and well-connected.

Urban Challenges

- Noise, traffic, and crowds might unsettle a Taurus seeking calm.
- Higher rents or property prices can force them into smaller, less cozy spaces.
- Less direct contact with nature, although city parks or balconies help.

Each Taurus must weigh these factors. Some might prefer a smaller town's slower pace, while others adapt to city life by creating a personal oasis at home.

Designing a Taurus-Friendly Interior

No matter where they live, Taurus can shape the interior of their home to match their sign's comfort-loving style:

Warm, Soft Lighting
Floor lamps or table lamps with warm-toned bulbs produce a cozy glow. Harsh overhead lights are usually avoided or softened with dimmers.

Textures and Fabrics
Plush rugs, throw blankets, or soft cushions bring tactile pleasure.

Taurus might pick natural materials like cotton, wool, or linen over synthetic.

Practical Kitchen
Since many Taurus individuals enjoy cooking, a functional kitchen with ample counter space and high-quality cookware is helpful. They might like to display attractive ceramics or jars, highlighting the kitchen's homey feel.

Art and Decor
Nature-themed artwork or prints of serene landscapes can reinforce calm. They may also appreciate decorative items that have sentimental or aesthetic value—like handmade pottery, wooden sculptures, or a houseplant corner.

A Place for Senses
Taurus often delights in gentle scents—candles, essential oils, or fresh flowers. Well-chosen scents, along with pleasing textures, engage multiple senses, which suits Taurus well.

With these touches, Taurus can transform any space, large or small, into a personal haven that reflects their steady temperament.

Work Environments for Taurus

While a home can be tailored for comfort, Taurus must also function in workplaces that might not always cater to them. Yet there are strategies for maintaining a grounded mindset:

Personal Desk Setup
If possible, Taurus might bring a small plant, a comfortable chair pad, or a calming photo. Even a discreet item like a stress ball can help.

Organized Workflow
Taurus likes clarity. Using labeled folders, a neat digital filing system, or well-structured planners can reduce stress. They may prefer a quiet corner of the office over a noisy open floor plan.

Routine
Breaking the day into predictable segments suits Taurus's style. They might plan tasks in advance, set times for lunch or breaks, and minimize last-minute changes.

Break Area
If the workplace has a lounge or garden, a Taurus can step away from the desk to calm their mind. If not, a short walk outside can serve the same purpose.

Remote or Hybrid Work
Some Taurus individuals thrive working from home, where they can control the environment. Having a dedicated home office with pleasing decor can boost productivity and well-being.

Even in a hectic professional setting, Taurus's habit of methodical organization and calming touches can maintain a sense of stability.

Vacation and Travel Destinations

Vacations or short getaways provide a chance for Taurus to recharge in surroundings that suit their leisurely pace and love for natural beauty.

Relaxing Nature Spots
Taurus might choose countryside retreats, lakeside cabins, or quiet beaches where they can soak up scenery without heavy tourist crowds.

Culinary-Focused Trips
Considering Taurus's enjoyment of good food, they may travel to regions famous for cuisine or vineyards—like Tuscany, Provence, or Napa Valley—to savor local flavors.

Spas and Wellness Centers
A spa resort with massages, hot springs, or gentle exercise options can be ideal for a Taurus seeking pampering. The slower schedule, comfortable accommodations, and tranquil settings align well with this sign.

Gentle Exploration
Taurus probably prefers moderate activities over high-adrenaline sports. A scenic train ride, a guided walk through vineyards, or a slow bike tour might appeal more than extreme adventures.

Cultural Immersion
If exploring a city, Taurus may want to linger in art museums, historic districts, or charming cafes instead of rushing to see every landmark.

By selecting trips that center on calm enjoyment, nature, and sensory pleasures, Taurus can make sure vacations truly restore their energy.

Adapting to Fast-Paced Cities

If a Taurus lives in or must spend time in a bustling metropolis, they can still find ways to remain grounded:

Incorporate Green Spaces
Seek out city parks or botanical gardens. Making time to visit these regularly gives Taurus a sense of nature amid the concrete.

Private Corners
Even in a crowded apartment, designating a small meditation nook or reading chair helps create mental space. A busy city can feel more manageable with a personal sanctuary at home.

Select Calm Neighborhoods
If finances allow, picking a quieter residential zone can reduce constant noise. Alternatively, using soundproof curtains or white noise machines can curb disruptive sounds.

Off-Peak Travel
Scheduling commutes outside rush hour, if possible, avoids crammed trains or traffic jams, letting Taurus keep a more relaxed routine.

Healthy Boundaries
In a place known for high speed, Taurus might learn to say no to constant outings or late-night events, preserving time for restful evenings and personal recharge.

Though city life can be challenging, these choices enable Taurus to enjoy urban advantages while staying true to their calmer pace.

Cultural Regions That Suit Taurus

While personal taste varies, certain parts of the world might particularly appeal to Taurus's senses:

European Countryside
Areas like rural France, Italy's rolling hills, or the English countryside can match Taurus's desire for scenic landscapes, good food, and quiet towns.

Coastal Retreats
Gentle coastlines with mild climates—like parts of Portugal or southern Australia—offer a blend of soothing ocean views and a laid-back pace.

Mountain Escapes
For Taurus who love fresh air and a stable environment, mountainous regions (like the Swiss Alps or Canada's Rockies) can feel calming, provided they can find comfortable lodgings.

Cultural Hubs with Gentle Vibes
Cities known for slower rhythms—like Kyoto in Japan or smaller Mediterranean towns—may delight a Taurus by combining cultural depth with an unhurried style.

Warm, Friendly Communities
Taurus also appreciates kindness and stable local customs. Regions with a tradition of hospitality, fresh local produce, and slower daily routines might perfectly align with this sign's preferences.

Again, each Taurus is unique, but these examples reflect typical sign values—comfort, a measured pace, and strong ties to the land.

Practical Tips for Moving or Relocating

When a Taurus considers a new home or city, they can apply these steps for a smoother transition:

Research Thoroughly
Taurus thrives on having facts. They might explore housing costs, local grocery options, and neighborhood features in detail before committing.

Visit if Possible
If finances allow, a short trip to the potential location can let Taurus feel the area's vibe, which is crucial for an earth sign sensitive to the environment.

Seek Nature Access
Whether it is a local park or proximity to the countryside, ensuring some greenery can keep Taurus balanced.

Budget for Quality
Taurus may want to rent or buy a place that is solidly built rather than the cheapest option. The long-term comfort usually justifies the cost if it fits their plan.

Create Familiar Routines
Upon arrival, Taurus can quickly set up a cozy corner or cook a favorite meal, anchoring themselves in the new space.

Following these guidelines can ease the anxiety of change, allowing Taurus to settle into a routine and feel at home faster.

Maintaining a Taurus Sanctuary on the Road

Even when not at home, Taurus might want to keep certain elements that make them feel safe:

Travel Comfort Kit
A small bag with personal touches—a soft scarf, a familiar tea blend, or a comforting scent spray—helps Taurus find calm in hotels or friend's houses.

Choose Lodgings Wisely
If traveling for business, picking a quiet hotel or Airbnb with comfy beds and less street noise can ensure better rest.

Routines in New Places
Even on a trip, Taurus can maintain small daily habits (like morning stretches or sipping a certain type of tea) to bring stability.

Walks in Nature or Parks
If the trip is to a crowded city, seeking out a local park or riverside walkway each morning or evening can reconnect Taurus to a sense of peace.

These steps help a Taurus preserve their sense of grounded well-being, no matter how temporary or unusual the setting.

Working in High-Stress Environments

Some Taurus individuals find themselves in fast-paced, high-stress workplaces—like tech startups, finance hubs, or emergency services. They can still craft calmer pockets:

Planning Breaks
Taurus might schedule micro-breaks for deep breaths or simple stretches. This can prevent overwhelm.

Quiet Communication
If constant chatter or open-concept offices are draining, they might ask for partial remote options or use noise-canceling headphones to keep focus.

Decor and Tools
A desk plant, a grounding crystal, or a personal notebook with soothing color designs can subtly support Taurus's need for comfort.

Practical Boundaries
Politely limiting after-hours work calls or organizing tasks to avoid last-minute chaos can ease tension.

Healthy Snacks
Having wholesome, satisfying snacks on hand can reduce hunger stress. A nutritious routine suits Taurus's emphasis on physical well-being.

While not always easy, these adaptations let Taurus keep a sense of stability in even the most hectic jobs.

Community and Social Environment

A suitable place is not just about the physical space—it also involves the people around you:

Stable Social Circles
Taurus typically values long-term friends or supportive neighbors. Living in a community where people engage steadily, rather than fleeting connections, can feel right.

Local Groups or Clubs
Joining gardening clubs, craft circles, or cooking classes can help a Taurus find like-minded folks. The environment becomes more welcoming when shared interests flourish.

Respect for Privacy
Taurus often needs personal downtime. A social environment where neighbors respect boundaries, or friends do not push for constant outings, suits them best.

Cultural Fit
Taurus can thrive in places with traditions or festivals focusing on nature, food, or comfort. This fosters a sense of belonging.

Clear, Practical Rules
In a condo board or neighborhood association, a Taurus might

appreciate well-defined guidelines that keep order. Haphazard or constantly changing rules may rattle their sense of security.

Choosing or shaping a social community that respects Taurus's slower style can elevate their daily contentment.

Seasonal Adjustments

Throughout the year, a Taurus may enjoy adjusting their environment to match seasonal shifts:

Spring Refresh
 This is Taurus season in many places (Northern Hemisphere). Adding fresh flowers or doing a mild home cleanup can energize the space.

Summer Airflow
 Light fabrics, open windows, and a comfortable outdoor seating area can help Taurus stay calm in warmer months.

Autumn Warmth
 Cozy blankets, earth-toned decor, and hearty meals mark a comforting fall environment. Taurus might bring in pumpkins or dried flowers for a seasonal touch.

Winter Nesting
 During colder months, layering soft rugs and cushions, and maybe a fireplace or scented candles, creates a snug haven. The sign's enjoyment of restful, warm nights is satisfied.

By gently altering their space each season, Taurus keeps the home environment fresh yet still reassuring.

Incorporating Sustainable Elements

As many Taurus folks care about long-lasting quality and nature, eco-friendly living might appeal:

Energy Efficiency
Installing LED lights, solar panels (if possible), or better insulation saves money and protects the environment—aligning with Taurus's practicality.

Local Sourcing
Buying furniture or decor from local artisans ensures strong craftsmanship and fewer shipping miles, matching Taurus's preference for tangible quality.

Composting and Gardening
Tending a small compost or herb garden helps Taurus feel close to the earth. They might also enjoy repurposing items to reduce waste.

Household Durability
Choosing items that last—like metal water bottles instead of plastic—reduces replacements and suits Taurus's steady approach.

Nature-Friendly Decor
Using plants that thrive indoors, plus sustainable wood or recycled materials, further ties Taurus to an earth-friendly mindset.

By integrating green choices, Taurus not only builds a stable environment but also feels they are contributing to the planet's well-being.

Cultural Traditions and Taurus Homes

In various cultures, traditions about home arrangement may pair well with Taurus's desire for harmony:

Feng Shui (China)
 This practice seeks balance in interior design through the arrangement of furniture and the flow of energy. Taurus might appreciate how it emphasizes comfort and stability with natural materials.

Vastu Shastra (India)
 Similar to Feng Shui, it focuses on harmonizing buildings with cosmic energy. A Taurus might adopt simple Vastu tips like placing furniture in stable, supportive directions.

Hygge (Denmark)
 This concept centers on coziness, warmth, and contentment—a dream approach for many Taurus individuals. Incorporating candles, soft textiles, and a relaxed atmosphere fosters well-being.

Other Regional Concepts
 From Japanese wabi-sabi to Mediterranean open-air courtyards, cultural design philosophies often resonate with Taurus's earthy preferences. They all emphasize calm, natural beauty, and timeless comfort.

A Taurus can draw on these global ideas to fine-tune their place, blending local traditions with universal desires for tranquility and ease.

Handling Overcrowded or Minimalist Trends

Society often oscillates between two extremes—living in cramped, overly decorated spaces or following strict minimalism. Taurus finds balance in between:

Avoiding Clutter
Too many objects can make a space feel claustrophobic. Taurus

benefits from regular tidying, focusing on fewer quality possessions that hold real value.

Resisting Extreme Minimalism
Going too sparse might rob a Taurus home of warmth. They can keep treasured items displayed, making sure the atmosphere remains inviting.

Functional Storage
A moderate approach—having enough storage so surfaces remain open, but not removing personal touches—keeps the environment calm yet characterful.

Personal Comfort Items
Whether it is a favorite blanket, art piece, or coffee mug collection, Taurus can keep items that spark everyday happiness.

Balance Above All
The aim is an uncluttered but cozy home, reflecting Taurus's preference for stable routines without a sense of emptiness.

By combining practicality and small pleasures, Taurus can steer clear of extremes that might disrupt their sense of ease.

Maintaining Harmony in Shared Spaces

Living with roommates, family, or a partner means Taurus cannot control every detail. They can still uphold a friendly environment:

Clear Communication
Taurus can gently share what helps them feel stable—like quiet morning hours or neat communal areas.

Accepting Differences
If others are less neat or more changeable, Taurus can compromise

on certain rooms or times. This balanced approach can reduce tension.

Designated Zones
Perhaps each person has a personal corner arranged to their taste. Taurus can keep their space calm without forcing the entire household to follow.

Shared Comfort Items
Investing in a comfy sofa or a communal kitchen gadget can please everyone and reflect Taurus's generosity.

Respect for Routine
Taurus's stable schedule might benefit others—like planning grocery trips or cleaning rosters. The household can function smoothly, thanks to Taurus's methodical help.

This approach merges the Taurus drive for order with the reality of co-living, supporting overall harmony.

Events, Parties, and Social Occasions

Taurus often likes hosting intimate gatherings rather than wild parties:

Home Entertaining
Inviting a few close friends over for a leisurely dinner suits Taurus. They can showcase good food, relaxed music, and a cozy vibe.

Decor for Guests
Soft lighting, a well-set table, and comfortable seating encourage guests to linger. Taurus may add a few fresh flowers or subtle scents to set the mood.

Menu Choices
Quality ingredients are key. A simple but delicious meal can make everyone feel cared for. Taurus is likely to choose dishes that comfort rather than show off complexity.

Calm Activities
Board games, low-key music, or unhurried conversation around the table can match Taurus's preference for deeper connections.

Avoiding Party Chaos
Taurus typically does not enjoy huge, chaotic gatherings. If forced to attend one, they might seek a quiet corner or limit their time to avoid overstimulation.

Such events let Taurus share their space's warmth, reflecting the sign's hospitable streak in an environment they can oversee.

The Emotional Link to Place

For Taurus, the bond with a place often goes beyond convenience to become a genuine emotional attachment:

Sentiment and Memories
A Taurus may hold onto a family home or an apartment they have lived in for years, feeling rooted in the memories made there.

Reluctance to Move
Their stable nature can make them hesitant to relocate unless they see a clear benefit. They prefer gradual, well-considered moves.

Home as Personal Refuge
More than a roof, the home is where they recharge. A disordered or constantly changing environment can drain them emotionally.

Investing Effort

Taurus may spend extra time and resources to customize a place just right—arranging furniture carefully, planting a garden, or repainting walls for the ideal color.

Celebrating Comfort

When the environment resonates, Taurus feels emotionally nurtured. This can help them approach challenges outside the home with more patience and grace.

By acknowledging this deeper attachment, Taurus can ensure they treat home and place decisions thoughtfully, respecting their sign's strong link to physical and emotional well-being.

CHAPTER 20: COMMON QUESTIONS ABOUT TAURUS

Throughout this book, we have explored the many facets of Taurus—the bull sign known for steady energy, practicality, and a fondness for comfort. Even so, people often have questions about what it truly means to be a Taurus or to live or work with someone who is. These questions can range from "Are Taurus folks really so stubborn?" to "How do I best connect with a Taurus friend or partner?" In this final chapter, we will address some of the most frequent inquiries that arise about Taurus. We will offer clear, simple answers rooted in general astrological ideas, while still reminding you that every person is different. By the end, you should have a deeper understanding of Taurus's common questions, helping you or those you care about make the most of this sign's steady, grounded nature.

"Do All Taurus Individuals Love Luxury and Possessions?"

Short Answer: Not necessarily. While many Taurus individuals enjoy quality items, comfort, and sometimes the finer things, they do not always chase after flashy luxuries.

Deeper Insight: Taurus is associated with the planet Venus, which can highlight a love of sensory enjoyment. Some interpret this as a desire for pleasant settings, tasty foods, or well-made products. However, "luxury" does not always mean high-priced items. It can mean carefully chosen clothing, a sturdy piece of furniture, or a warm blanket that lasts for years. The main point is practicality: a

Taurus might save up for something they truly value rather than spending impulsively on trendy or showy things.

Useful Tip: If you see a Taurus investing in something that seems expensive, they are often looking for durability and reliability, not just a brand name. Many are fine with a simpler lifestyle if it fits their standard of comfort and practicality.

"Why Are Taurus Folks Described as Stubborn?"

Short Answer: They can be firm and prefer stability, so when they make a choice, they do not give it up easily. But there is more nuance than just being "stubborn."

Deeper Insight: Taurus is a fixed sign, meaning once they latch onto an idea or routine, it might be hard for them to switch. This can become a strength, as they have persistence to keep going when others quit. On the other hand, if they remain locked into a narrow approach long after conditions change, it can cause friction.

Managing Stubbornness: Communication helps. Rather than pushing a Taurus aggressively, calmly explain why another approach might benefit them. They typically respond better to polite, logical discussions than to sudden demands. If a Taurus feels respected, they can slowly adapt.

Positive Side: This "stubbornness" can show up as loyalty or dedication when it matters most—like staying with a friend through tough times. They might take a while to open to change, but they can handle new ideas if given space and time.

"Are Taurus Individuals Really Lazy or Slow?"

Short Answer: They are not necessarily lazy; they simply move at a measured pace. They prefer to ensure tasks are done right, avoiding rushed actions.

Deeper Insight: Taurus can be careful and methodical, which is sometimes confused with slowness. In fact, many Taurus folks are hard workers who see projects through to completion. They also place importance on rest, wanting to avoid burnout. This balanced approach can appear lazy to someone who wants everything done instantly, but in truth, it often leads to steady, high-quality results.

Practical Example: A Taurus employee might take longer to learn a new skill thoroughly, but once mastered, they perform consistently and rarely make careless mistakes. The same pattern applies in personal hobbies, where they favor step-by-step mastery rather than quick attempts.

Finding Balance: While caution is good, a Taurus can improve by recognizing moments when speed is needed. If a situation demands quick decisions, trying small steps or letting others guide some changes can keep them from falling behind.

"Do Taurus People Only Care About Money?"

Short Answer: Not at all. They do prioritize financial stability, but it is usually tied to a need for security and comfort rather than pure greed.

Deeper Insight: Financial stability for Taurus is about feeling safe. They prefer to know bills are covered, savings are set aside, and basic comforts are ensured. They are typically cautious with money, wanting to avoid sudden financial shocks. This can come off as materialistic if viewed from the outside, but for many Taurus individuals, money is a practical tool rather than a symbol of status.

Managing Money: Taurus might set budgets, invest in stable options, and keep track of expenses more carefully than some other signs. However, many also treat themselves to small pleasures—like a good meal or a sturdy pair of shoes—seeing it as a worthy reward for their consistent effort.

Finding a Middle Ground: If a Taurus becomes overly focused on saving or possessions, they can remind themselves that experiences, relationships, and personal growth also enrich life. Money is useful, but genuine fulfillment can come from deeper sources, too.

"How Can I Best Communicate with a Taurus?"

Short Answer: Use clear, calm, and respectful dialogue. Show them you have thought things through rather than demanding abrupt changes.

Deeper Insight: Taurus can be somewhat private, especially early in relationships. They might not share all feelings at once. Hence, building trust gradually works best. Also, they often dislike loud arguments or overly emotional confrontations. A calm tone, direct facts, and practical solutions can help them see your point.

Tips for Conversations:

- **Offer Time to Process**: If you present a new idea, let them think about it for a bit before expecting a final answer.
- **Use Practical Examples**: Show how a suggestion will actually help them or others in real ways.
- **Stay Gentle**: If you push too hard, they might dig in their heels. Slow, steady dialogue is more effective.

Listening Skills: Remember, Taurus typically listens carefully. Even if they do not jump to confirm or reject, they often weigh your words and come back with their thoughts later.

"What About Taurus in Friendships?"

Short Answer: They tend to be loyal, consistent friends who prefer smaller, close circles over large gatherings.

Deeper Insight: A Taurus friend may not be the life of the party, but they will stand by you if you need support. They might invite you for a home-cooked meal or watch a comforting movie rather than going to loud clubs. Their reliability is a strong asset: if they promise help, they follow through.

Social Settings: They can enjoy group events if the environment is not chaotic. If everything is too rowdy, they might slip away to a quieter corner. Good friends respect this preference for calmer spaces.

Maintaining Friendship: Reaching out regularly with simple gestures—like checking in or sharing a meal—can keep the bond strong. Taurus values stable contact over sporadic, dramatic meetups.

"How Does Taurus Handle Romantic Relationships?"

Short Answer: Taurus often looks for commitment, honesty, and comfort. They appreciate shared routines and consistent emotional support.

Deeper Insight: In romance, Taurus is known for being affectionate once trust is established. They might show love through practical acts—cooking a favorite dish, helping fix things around the house, or giving a thoughtful present. They tend to be patient with a partner's ups and downs, as long as they feel secure themselves.

Challenges: If a partner wants constant novelty, Taurus may struggle with rapid changes. They can adapt, but prefer clear reasons and gentle pacing. Also, if arguments get heated or emotional extremes occur often, a Taurus might withdraw to avoid conflict overload.

Strengths: They can create a warm, stable home life, enjoying physical closeness and shared comforts. Many see them as a rock in relationships, offering lasting support and calm.

"Are Taurus Individuals Really Foodies?"

Short Answer: Quite a few are, due to their sign's fondness for sensory pleasure and comfort. But it varies by person.

Deeper Insight: Taurus is often tagged as a lover of good meals and cozy gatherings. This is not a rule for every single Taurus, but many do gain pleasure from cooking, tasting new dishes, or even discovering the best local bakery. It ties back to how they experience the world through senses—taste included.

Healthy Balance: A Taurus might need to watch portion sizes or unhealthy snacking if they find big comfort in food. However, if they approach meals mindfully and enjoy fresh, quality ingredients, it can be a fulfilling pastime.

Bonding Through Food: Cooking a meal for loved ones or trying local cuisine while traveling can be prime ways a Taurus shares enjoyment with others. It supports their desire for slow, steady satisfaction in daily life.

"How Do Taurus People React Under Pressure?"

Short Answer: They usually stay calm on the outside, handling stress with measured steps. But if pushed too far, they can show surprising force.

Deeper Insight: Taurus tends to keep an even temper for a long time. They manage problems by seeking practical solutions, often in a slow, step-by-step manner. If a conflict escalates beyond reason, they may become quite firm or even angry, but that is typically a last resort.

Stress Relief: Activities like going for a walk, spending time in a tranquil environment, or enjoying a favorite hobby can help them cope. Some might talk to a close friend or partner if they feel truly overwhelmed, though they might not share every detail right away.

Advice for Others: If you see a Taurus under pressure, be patient and offer to help in concrete ways—like assisting with tasks or giving them space to process. Encouraging them to break challenges into smaller parts suits their practical nature.

"How Does Taurus Fare in Careers or Jobs?"

Short Answer: They excel in roles requiring steady effort, attention to detail, and consistent output. They might avoid jobs with constant chaos or risk.

Deeper Insight: Taurus thrives when they can learn a skill thoroughly, then apply it day after day. They often become the dependable pillar of a team or office, rarely missing deadlines. Fields involving finance, design, gardening, cooking, construction, or anything else that merges practicality with tangible results might appeal.

Leadership Style: As managers, Taurus may be methodical, setting clear rules. They expect people to do what they said they would. Sometimes, they might resist adopting brand-new methods without proof those methods work. However, they are usually fair and grounded, giving team members a sense of stability.

Work Drawbacks: If a job requires constant sudden changes or if the environment is loud and disorganized, a Taurus can feel drained. Finding ways to keep routines or at least a calm personal workspace can help them adapt better in such fields.

"Is Taurus Always Loyal?"

Short Answer: Often, yes. Taurus is famed for loyalty, but as with any sign, it depends on personal values and the situation.

Deeper Insight: If a Taurus cares about you and sees a real bond, they tend to stand by you through thick and thin. This is part of their fixed-sign nature: once committed, they do not back away easily. However, loyalty does not mean they will stay in a situation forever if they feel deeply betrayed or unsafe.

Balance: Sometimes, Taurus's loyalty can border on staying too long in an unhealthy situation. Learning when to step away is important. Yet, for the most part, their dedication is seen as a strong plus, and many appreciate having a Taurus friend or partner for that reason.

"What Are Taurus's Biggest Weaknesses?"

Short Answer: Stubbornness, reluctance to change, and the tendency to rely heavily on familiar comforts can pose challenges.

Deeper Insight: Because Taurus likes predictability, they can resist necessary changes for too long, causing missed chances or letting problems fester. They might also cling to routines that no longer serve them. If their desire for comfort goes extreme, they may avoid growth or fail to step out of a safe zone, which could hamper personal or professional development.

Improving on Weaknesses:

- **Small Steps**: Easing into new experiences one bit at a time can help them handle change better.

- **Getting Feedback**: Listening to close friends or mentors can provide a reality check when they are stuck in an unhelpful pattern.

- **Mindful Self-Care**: Balancing comfort with a push to explore can maintain the best of both worlds.

"How Does Taurus Compare to Other Earth Signs?"

Short Answer: All earth signs value practicality, but each has a unique flavor. Taurus is typically more about steady growth and comfort, Virgo tends to be more detail-oriented, and Capricorn is often goal-driven.

Taurus vs. Virgo: Virgo might be faster at noticing small errors and can be more critical or analytical. Taurus is less about daily detailed adjustments and more about the consistent buildup of comfort over time.

Taurus vs. Capricorn: Capricorn focuses on climbing the career or social ladder, often setting long-term goals. Taurus is also ambitious, but usually in a personal, stable way. They might say, "I want a home and a modest savings," whereas Capricorn might chase a major leadership role or broad success.

Shared Traits: All three earth signs have a love for tangible results, reliability, and a direct approach. They can work well together, forming a practical team that turns ideas into reality.

"Do Taurus Individuals Connect Easily with Nature?"

Short Answer: They often do, given the sign's earth element. Many enjoy gardening, walks, or scenic travel.

Deeper Insight: Because Taurus is associated with physical reality, being in nature can feel soothing and recharging. It might be a small hobby—like tending houseplants or strolling in the park—or a bigger project, like caring for a home garden. Touching soil, observing green spaces, or hearing birds can ground them.

Encouraging the Connection: If a Taurus seems stressed, gently nudging them to step outside or cultivate a few potted herbs might help them reset. They do not always need wild adventures—sometimes the simplest contact with nature brings comfort.

"Are Taurus Folks Good at Creative or Artistic Pursuits?"

Short Answer: Yes, many are, though they favor practical art or something with a tangible outcome. They can be quite creative in a slow, detail-focused way.

Deeper Insight: Taurus is ruled by Venus, the planet linked to beauty. Some Taurus people thrive in music, painting, pottery, cooking, or design. They are apt to approach such arts methodically, learning step by step until they master techniques. They might not chase spontaneous bursts of creativity as much as a sign like Aries or Gemini, but the final product can be polished and refined.

Typical Styles:

- **Music**: They may enjoy slower melodies or classical pieces that convey warmth.

- **Visual Arts**: They often prefer realistic or nature-themed art, focusing on textures and earthy colors.

- **Culinary Arts**: Cooking or baking is a strong area for some Taurus individuals, blending creativity with practical nourishment.

"Which Signs Are Most Compatible with Taurus?"

Short Answer: Traditional astrology suggests Taurus pairs well with fellow earth signs (Virgo, Capricorn) and certain water signs (Cancer, Pisces, Scorpio). But actual compatibility depends on full birth charts and personalities.

Deeper Insight:

- **Virgo, Capricorn**: They share Taurus's grounded outlook, often creating stable relationships built on mutual goals.
- **Cancer, Pisces**: Water signs can balance Taurus's practicality with emotional depth, leading to nurturing bonds. Scorpio, the opposite sign, can bring passion or power struggles, depending on mutual respect.

Other Combinations: Taurus can get along with any sign if they find shared interests and respect each other's styles. Fire or air signs might challenge Taurus's routine, but it can be a chance to grow.

Key Factor: Rather than focusing solely on "best sign," it helps to look for calm communication, shared values, and a willingness to adapt gently.

"How Can Taurus Improve Their Flexibility?"

Short Answer: By trying small, low-risk changes and reminding themselves that some adjustments can lead to better stability in the long run.

Concrete Steps:

- **Try Something New Weekly**: Maybe a different meal or a new route home. Small shifts teach Taurus that change is not always negative.
- **Set Realistic Goals**: Instead of leaping into big transformations, a Taurus can break them into tiny steps. For instance, if they want to adopt a new habit, they can start with five minutes a day.
- **Look at Positive Outcomes**: Listing how changes have helped in the past can reassure them that not all changes disrupt comfort.
- **Ask for Trusted Support**: Close friends can gently encourage them, providing stable companionship as they explore fresh experiences.

This approach ensures Taurus remains steady but does not miss out on growth opportunities.

"Is a Taurus Likely to Overindulge?"

Short Answer: There is a risk of overdoing comforts—be it food, relaxation, or shopping. However, a balanced Taurus can manage these temptations with sensible measures.

Why the Tendency?: The sign's love of good food or soothing items can lean into indulgence if not kept in check. Sometimes stress leads them to seek comfort in treats or impulse buying.

Preventive Measures:

- **Mindful Eating**: Focusing on flavor and portion size instead of mindless snacking can help.
- **Budget Limits**: Setting spending rules and saving goals supports their security desires without going overboard.
- **Replacing Overindulgences**: Finding other soothing methods—like reading, gentle exercise, or craft hobbies—can limit reliance on snacks or shopping.

Balance remains key. A Taurus can enjoy pleasures but also guard against habits that might harm overall well-being.

"How Do I Support a Taurus Who Feels Stressed or Unsettled?"

Short Answer: Offer practical help, a calm presence, and reassurance of stability. Avoid forcing swift solutions or bombarding them with advice.

Deeper Insight: A stressed Taurus may become quieter or even appear stubborn. They need time to process the root cause. Providing a listening ear, or assisting with small tasks, can help them regain a sense of order.

Suggestions:

- **Create a Soothing Environment**: Lower the noise, tidy up, or bring them a comforting blanket or beverage.
- **Gently Discuss Options**: Lay out possible solutions step by step. Let them pick which path feels most secure.

- **Encourage Short Breaks**: A walk in fresh air or a peaceful corner can calm racing thoughts.
- **Respect Their Pace**: If they require a bit of silence or alone time, do not take it personally.

By being patient and supportive, you can help them find their footing again.

"Are All Taurus People the Same?"

Short Answer: Definitely not. Each Taurus has a unique full birth chart, plus personal experiences shaping their character.

Deeper Insight: While sun signs are a handy shortcut, every person is influenced by upbringing, culture, and personal choices. Some Taurus individuals will show strong classic traits—like routine and calm—whereas others, due to their moon, rising sign, or life experiences, may act more spontaneously or be quite open to change.

Why Variations Occur:

- **Family Environment**: A Taurus raised in a hectic city might learn to adapt more quickly.
- **Cultural Beliefs**: Different societies emphasize different values, possibly guiding a Taurus to behave outside typical sign stereotypes.
- **Personal Growth**: Over time, a Taurus can refine or shift how they express their sign's strengths, working on any weaknesses.

Ultimately, while Taurus offers a broad template of traits—stability, preference for comfort, and groundedness—each person's path is distinct.

Conclusion

Common questions about Taurus often revolve around the same core topics: is every Taurus stubborn, slow, or fond of physical comforts? Do they struggle with change, or is that just a rumor? How do they handle relationships, work, and everyday stress? The answers show that Taurus does indeed bring strong qualities of steadiness, patience, and reliability, along with certain potential pitfalls, such as stubbornness or resisting swift changes. Yet, each Taurus remains an individual, shaped by personal and cultural factors.

This final chapter ties together many threads explored throughout the book. From how Taurus interacts with money and work, to how they form friendships or romance, to how they manage day-to-day living—these commonly asked questions boil down to a central theme: Taurus strives for a secure, comfortable, and grounded life. They find peace when their environment, schedules, and social bonds align with a calm, practical outlook. By appreciating both the sign's gentle warmth and its firm boundaries, friends, family, and Taurus themselves can enjoy healthy, stable connections.

Above all, whether you see Taurus as a precise astrological fact or a guiding symbol, the best approach is to respect each person's unique blend of traits. When you meet a Taurus or discover you share this sign's qualities, remember that behind the typical descriptions (loyal, comfort-loving, patient) stands a whole human being, shaped by experiences and personal growth. Tapping into that deeper understanding fosters respect, empathy, and genuine harmony—just like the calm, nurturing spirit that Taurus aims to bring into daily life.

Help Us Share Your Thoughts!

Dear reader,

Thank you for spending your time with this book. We hope it brought you enjoyment and a few new ideas to think about. If there was anything that didn't work for you, or if you have suggestions on how we can improve, please let us know at **kontakt@skriuwer.com**. Your feedback means a lot to us and helps us make our books even better.

If you enjoyed this book, we would be very grateful if you left a review on the site where you purchased it. Your review not only helps other readers find our books, but also encourages us to keep creating more stories and materials that you'll love.

By choosing Skriuwer, you're also supporting **Frisian**—a minority language mainly spoken in the northern Netherlands. Although **Frisian** has a rich history, the number of speakers is shrinking, and it's at risk of dying out. Your purchase helps fund resources to preserve and promote this language, such as educational programs and learning tools. If you'd like to learn more about Frisian or even start learning it yourself, please visit **www.learnfrisian.com**.

Thank you for being part of our community. We look forward to sharing more books with you in the future.

Warm regards,
The Skriuwer Team

www.ingramcontent.com/pod-product-compliance
Lightning Source LLC
LaVergne TN
LVHW012035070526
838202LV00056B/5503